REVELATION

A Devotional Commentary

GENERAL EDITOR

Leo Zanchettin

The Word Among Us Press
9639 Doctor Perry Road
Ijamsville, Maryland 21754
www.wordamongus.org

11 10 09 08 07   1 2 3 4 5

ISBN: 978-1-59325-106-2

Scripture passages contained herein are from the New Revised Standard Version Bible: Catholic Edition, copyright © 1989, 1993 Division of Christian Education of the National Council of the Churches of Christ in the United States. All rights reserved. Used with permission. Scripture passages in Fr. Henry Wansbrough's article, "The 'Day of the Lord,'" are his own translation.

Cover design by David Crosson
Nicholas of Verdun (c.1150-1205)
Angels of the Ressurection, from the Verdun Altar.
Enamel plaque in chempleve technique on gilded copper, begun 1181.
Location : Sammlungen des Stiftes, Klosterneuburg Abbey, Austria
Photo Credit: Erich Lessing/Art Resource, NY

Made and printed in the United States of America

Library of Congress Control Number: 2007930402

Table of Contents

Acknowledgments

I want to thank everyone who has made this commentary possible, especially all of the writers who contributed meditations. Some of the meditations appearing in this book were initially developed for *The Word Among Us* monthly publication, and I am grateful to these writers for granting us permission to reprint their work. I also want to thank Fr. Joseph Mindling, OFM Cap, and Fr. Henry Wansbrough, OSB, for contributing the opening chapters that set the stage for the commentary that follows. A special note of thanks also goes to Jill Boughton, Bob French, Hallie Riedel, and Greg Roa for their considerable contributions to the meditations. Thanks, too, go to Margaret Procario for her work of editing of the manuscript, and to Kathy Mayne for gathering and collating much of the material that went into this book. Finally, I want to thank Patricia Mitchell, editor of The Word Among Us Press, for her patience and persistence in seeing this project through to its completion. May the Lord abundantly bless each of them!

Leo Zanchettin

Preface

Home Sweet Home
Fixing Our Eyes on Our Ultimate Goal

Leo Zanchettin

Horizons have always enthralled me. I love going to the beach—but not to lie out in the sun or swim in the surf or collect seashells. I go just to stand at the water's edge and stare into the distance, looking at the point where the ocean meets the sky. I am also fascinated with the nighttime sky. In an almost eerie way, I find comfort gazing into that vast expanse of space and imagining what it must be like out there. If I had the time and patience, I would buy a telescope and learn all about astronomy. In a similar way, I love standing in the middle of an old, dense forest, surrounded by nothing but the quiet nobility of so many ancient trees.

Somehow these natural, untamed settings give me a sense of being "home," even though I grew up in and continue to live in the manicured, predictable, and decidedly tame world of suburbia. It's as if part of me knows that this manufactured and synthetic world of strip malls, multiplex theaters, and pocket parks doesn't do justice to who we really are and what our lives are really about. Going to the beach or the woods or gazing into the starry night always makes me feel as if I am coming out of exile and returning to my true homeland.

Perhaps this is why I have always been intrigued by the Book of Revelation. In chapter after chapter, this book puts us in touch with a much larger—and far more glorious—realm than the world we have manufactured for ourselves. Even as it tells the story of an epic battle at the end of time, Revelation gives us regular glimpses into our true home. It shows us One who is seated on a dazzling throne—the Father who created us. It shows us a glorified Lamb still bearing the marks of his crucifixion—Jesus, who died and rose for us. It tells us about the four living creatures and twelve elders and countless angels bowing down in adoration—figures who speak of God's eternity, majesty, and mystery. And it shows us innumerable saints singing the glory of the Lord—our brothers and sisters who have gone before us and who continue to intercede for us.

When you think about it, Revelation shows us the ultimate horizon. And in the process, it creates in us a sense of belonging, a conviction that our hearts belong *there*, not *here*. The images, language, and story line in this book all combine to tell us that we were made for heaven, and that no matter how hard we try to make our home in this world, the fulfillment we long for won't come until we cross the last threshold and enter heaven. Then will our restless hearts finally find the peace they have been looking for.

And so, the goal of this commentary is not to decode every image and symbol, give you a guide to predicting the future, or tell you exactly how the second coming will come about. Neither is it to tell you where other interpretations of Revelation are right or wrong. No, our goal is to help lift up your heart with a vision of heaven. It is to help you come before the throne of God in your own prayer so that you can find your true home in Christ. Of course, we hope that you learn something about the Bible and our Catholic faith along the way.

As you read and pray through the meditations in this commentary, lift up your eyes! Fix your gaze on Jesus, who is not only your risen Lord but your soon and coming King as well. Know that he didn't redeem you just so that your sins could be forgiven. He did it so that you could be united with him forever in an embrace of perfect, unconditional love. Let this truth—this promise of salvation—move you to a life of deeper trust in him, deeper reverence for his people, and deeper obedience to his ways. Jesus is coming back, and when he does appear, every glorious horizon and landscape we now know will pale in comparison to the beauty and the glory that will be our new home.

The End Is Near . . . Or Is It?

"Decoding" the Book of Revelation

THE END IS NEAR . . . OR IS IT?

Introduction

The End Is Near . . . Or Is It?
"Decoding" the Book of Revelation

Rev. Joseph Mindling, OFM Cap

In recent years, the Book of Revelation and its dramatic end-of-the-world imagery have attracted the attention of thousands of fundamentalist believers. At the same time, thousands of other believers have deliberately avoided this book, which they find both confusing and unsettling.

It's ironic that both of these reactions often stem from a similar set of misunderstandings. A widespread but mistaken presupposition is that Revelation contains secret, coded messages giving the dates and details of cataclysmic events just around the corner. Another reading holds that certain characters in the book are meant to represent secular or church leaders from later periods. In different groups, for instance, the Antichrist has been identified with both Adolf Hitler and the pope.

Interpretations like those are not only wildly off the mark, they also keep us from grasping what this book is really supposed to be: a rich source of teaching and encouragement for believers in every age. So let's take a look at the Book of Revelation in a way that will help us move beyond these negative notions. With the help of the Spirit, let's try to uncover a more balanced—and a far more hopeful—approach to what God wants to tell us in this book.

Mixed-Up Methods?

Revelation is not the only literary work that has been the subject of wild misinterpretation. One of the most famous cases of misinterpretation occurred on October 30, 1938, when a radio adaptation of the science fiction novel *The War of the Worlds* was broadcast in the United States. The broadcast—which presented the story of a fictitious invasion from Mars as if it were an actual news report—caused a large number of listeners who had missed the introduction to panic, thinking that Martians really had landed in New Jersey and were killing everyone in sight. People in 1938 were familiar both with science fiction dramas and actual news reporting. But this episode showed how easily one type of program could get confused for another, producing unintended and embarrassing results!

Living two thousand years ago, our ancestors in the faith would hardly have recognized these two forms of communication. Still, they had their own kinds of communication that are as unfamiliar to us as documentaries and soap operas would have been to them. The Book of Revelation is a prime example. "Apocalyptic" literature—as it has come to be called—was quite familiar to first-century Christians and Jews. After all, it had already been around for about two hundred years. Unfortunately, there is no modern equivalent to this type of writing, so we may not know exactly how to respond when we encounter it ourselves.

The only other surviving writings that are exclusively apocalyptic in style come from outside the Bible and are usually unfamiliar to anyone but scholars in the field. Nevertheless, numerous other Scripture passages have many of the same distinctive characteristics. Most are in the Old Testament, in passages such as Daniel 7-12; Isaiah 24-27; Ezekiel 38-39; Joel 1-2; and Zechariah 9-14. There are also some brief apocalyptic passages in the New Testament, including Mark 13:5-37; Matthew 24:4-36; and Luke 21:8-36; as well as in several of the Pauline letters, including Romans 13:11-14; 1 Corinthians 15; 2 Corinthians 12; 1 Thessalonians 4; and 2 Thessalonians 2. In these passages, we can see themes similar to those in Revelation, especially the theme of God intervening in our world to bring good out of evil and establish his eternal kingdom.

Crisis Response

Where did this kind of writing come from? Apocalyptic literature arose as faithful Jews and Christians sought to respond to the experience of either external persecution or some internal crisis of faith. The authors of this type of literature were trying to look at their crises from a "God's-eye" perspective. They wanted to interpret the concrete circumstances of their lives in terms of the universal struggle between good and evil—and when they did, they relied upon images, story lines, and symbols that would have been relevant to other believers in their era.

So what makes a written work apocalyptic? And how can these other writings help us better understand the Book of Revelation? All apocalyptic writings share two characteristics: a vividly portrayed shift from the world as we know it to an end-times climax, and a consideration of the way present beliefs and conduct affect our final destiny.

The Future as a Guaranteed Reality

Like the other apocalypses that were written during the same time, the Book of Revelation is indeed concerned with the future—but not with laying out concrete dates and details. Rather, John—as the author of Revelation identifies himself—sought to present the future as a guaranteed reality that will come about as a result of choices made in the present. By dramatizing the punishments that await the unfaithful and assuring the righteous of ultimate victory—as well as rewards that will replace their current sufferings—

John wanted to bolster his readers' perseverance and help turn those still in darkness and distress toward the light of Christ.

Despite their many similarities, the New Testament Book of Revelation is also strikingly different from all of its Old Testament and non-biblical predecessors in one very important way. At the heart of Revelation stands Jesus Christ, the Savior and Messiah who is central in all of God's cosmic plans to fill us with divine life and to bring us into his heavenly kingdom. As a result, every major aspect of this book that parallels other apocalyptic writings does so in a way that lifts the content—as well as the readers—into a new dimension.

In most apocalyptic works, the central narrator comes in touch with the heavenly realm through a dream or by the appearance of an angelic messenger. By contrast, John's initial encounter is with the risen Christ himself, who is mysteriously glorified yet still fully human. Although Jesus now holds the stars in his hands (Revelation 2:1), all that he says and does in this book shows how deeply interested he is in the lives of his faithful followers. This Jesus is the same Galilean who moved among his flock, pasturing, reproving, doing whatever their well-being required—even dying on a cross.

It is only after this connection with the familiar, approachable Jesus has been made clear that the fuller picture unfolds. This Good Shepherd shows himself to be the divine Lamb, once slain but now fully alive and enthroned with God. And in the light of the glory of God and the Lamb, the distracting veil of "the way things appear" is pulled aside to reveal what is really going on—and what is of lasting, even everlasting, importance.

Of course, this kind of thinking would have been considered just short of treason during the persecutions of the early church. But don't we also live in a world that can be quite hostile to the values of our religious heritage? In some countries, Christians are subjected to physical violence as blatant as that of the Roman persecutions. In other places, the campaign to remove mention of God from the public forum and to intimidate religious leaders from speaking out in defense of gospel values is shamelessly aggressive. Perhaps it is time to take a fresh look at these closing pages of the New Testament. Maybe they have more to say to us and to our age than we might have suspected.

Come, Lord Jesus!

From a large-scale perspective, the Book of Revelation was clearly written to raise our awareness of the way sin displeases God. Its sometimes awesome descriptions of both crime and punishment harness our imaginations and reinforce our disdain for the ugliness of moral evil. Revelation also uses literary drama to assure us that God really is aware of the unmerited suffering that comes from human evildoing. He sees all the suffering and trials of his people, and he promises to right all wrongs when he comes again to usher in his final victory.

On a more personal level, Revelation can help us see our lives in a new light. By depicting God's loyal followers as those who have survived a "great ordeal" by relying on his power and protection, it shows us that we too can stand firm with hope and confidence. Truths like this have the power to strengthen and encourage that inner part of us where our hopes, fears, dreams, and ability to trust are rooted.

What's more, the songs that these followers of the Lamb sing can touch us deeply. They show us that we can enter into the spirit of this book by making these prayers our own, as we join with the saints in their endless hymns of praise and adoration. The simple prayers that appear throughout the Book of Revelation are prayers that we can offer to the Lord at any point in our day. And as we do, we too will find our hearts lifted up.

Finally, the Book of Revelation can both challenge and console us when we think about our own death. For it is then, when we have passed from earth to heaven, that we will finally be united with the celestial chorus and sing the song that no one can learn "except the one hundred forty-four thousand who have been redeemed from the earth" (Revelation 14:3).

All of these ways of looking at Revelation show us that this book is not simply a curious piece of writing that has to be decoded. Far from it, Revelation is an inspired text in which God speaks to our hearts and raises our hopes and expectations. Ultimately, we know that we have made progress when reading this book moves us to cry out, in union with all the heavenly hosts, "Amen! Come, Lord Jesus!"

A Brief Outline of Revelation

Because Revelation is characterized by very graphic scenarios and often abrupt transitions, it is helpful to keep track in a Bible of where these materials come from, so that they don't seem to hang in the air as disconnected snippets. So let's review the thought flow of the brief introduction, the narrative segments, and the epilogue that work together to make up the whole of Revelation.

1. The Introduction and the Opening Encounter with Christ— Revelation 1:1–3:22

The Book of Revelation begins with two simple paragraphs. The first sets out the purpose of the book, and the second creates a doctrinal framework through a poetic summary of several significant beliefs that the early church professed about Jesus.

The narrative section begins with a description of the risen Christ, surrounded by symbols of divine sovereignty, appearing to John. In this vision, Jesus tells him to write down prophetic messages—challenging but also reassuring—to seven churches. These letters contain interesting historical details, but more important, they deliver the overarching message of Revelation: "Remain true to your call. Give no ground to the forces of evil. The challenges and sufferings you face are daunting, but a share in the Lord's permanent victory is guaranteed for everyone who perseveres."

2. The Heavenly Court and the Sealed Scroll—Revelation 4:1–5:14

Next, John is shown the heavenly court where God shares his divine throne with Jesus, who appears in the form of a slain but risen Lamb. Together, both Jesus and the Father receive the adoration of ranks of worshippers: twenty-four elders, myriads of angels, a multitude of saints clothed in white, and four "living creatures"—mysterious figures reminiscent of those in Ezekiel 1:5-21. In his right hand, God holds a scroll containing his divine plan, which determines the flow and outcome of all the events of creation. The only one worthy of revealing the contents of this scroll is the Lamb, who accepts it amid songs of praise by the heavenly choirs.

3. The Perennial Conflict Between God and Evil—Revelation 6:1–9:21

The breaking open of the seals binding the scroll exposes how seriously human history has been marred by the disobedience of the wicked, who persecute Jesus' followers. It also shows that God has heard the prayers of those suffering persecution. Not one to turn a blind eye, he is already punishing the evil in the world, especially through devastating natural disasters. Unfortunately, the wicked stubbornly ignore wave after wave of these chastisements and continue in their rebellion and persecution.

4. The Symbolic Signs of the Imminent End—Revelation 10:1–11:19

At length, an angel appears with a second, smaller scroll, which John is commanded to eat. He discovers that even though it tastes sweet in his mouth, the scroll turns his stomach bitter. This episode symbolizes John's commission to announce that all of history is approaching its momentous climax, and that victory will overshadow defeat once and for all. Other symbolic actions confirm how close this victory is: the measurement of the temple, the appearance of two final prophets, and a cry of heavenly voices announcing that God has already taken over control of "the kingdom of the world" (Revelation 11:15). And with that, the scene changes as the heavenly temple is opened, signaling the critical turning point in the story.

5. The Climactic Conflict—Revelation 12:1–14:20

Beginning in Chapter 12, we see a vision of a great battle that will conclude the flow of history as we know it and inaugurate the final age. The powers of evil, lurking behind the sinful conduct of the earlier chapters, now assume a name and a face. Satan appears in the form of a ravenous, red dragon—and he is not alone. Two malevolent henchmen also appear, depicted as hideous beasts who coerce people by deceit and intimidation to worship the dragon. Marshaled against them is the Lamb, with his army of 144,000 followers and countless angelic troops under the leadership of the archangel Michael.

6. The Eschatological Battle—Revelation 15:1–22:5

Next comes an extended battle, interspersed with songs in praise of the victorious and true God. Mounted on a white horse, Jesus is depicted as the glorious winner who utterly humiliates and destroys "Babylon"—symbol of the earthly home of the powers of evil. Those who joined with the forces of good are granted access to the new Jerusalem, a paradise that is free from tears, death, pain, ugliness, and even the dark of night.

8. The Epilogue: The Renewed Call for Readiness—Revelation 22:6–21

The saga concludes by returning to John and his angelic guide. He cautions us to heed the words of the book and to be prepared for Jesus' imminent return in glory—the central event that has been figuratively described throughout the pages of this book.

How to Read—And How Not to Read—Revelation

Read almost any passage from this inspired book, and you will be brought into contact with that kaleidoscope of word-pictures that make up much of its distinctive style: vibrant colors, theologically significant numbers, the use of animals as agents of good and evil, and imagery taken from the astronomy of the day. We are blessed to have access to translations that provide brief explanations for most of these symbols right in our Bibles. Steadily learning more about these passages not only enhances our understanding, it helps us hear God speak to us more personally and directly when we hear them proclaimed at Mass.

If we keep in mind the poetic nature of the Book of Revelation, we will be careful not to think of it as a set of specific predictions or a manual of technological instructions. A text like this is not meant to serve as an exact-scale map of heaven or to supply secret information to a favored few who are good at deciphering hidden religious codes. In fact, Jesus tells us that no mortal person—and not even the angels—can know the specific time of the end of the world (Mark 13:32, Matthew 24:36; Luke 12:40). The Book of Revelation was never intended to be a biblical crystal ball. Instead, when approached with respect for centuries of scriptural tradition, inspired apocalyptic literature can affect us in far more profound ways.

The "Day of the Lord"

The Place of Revelation in an
Ancient Biblical Tradition

The "Day of the Lord"

The "Day of the Lord"
The Place of Revelation in an Ancient Biblical Tradition

Rev. Henry Wansbrough, OSB

Over the years, the Book of Revelation has been read as allegory, as settled prophecy, and as a description of the state of the early church during a time of persecution. But no matter how it is interpreted, one thing is clear: Revelation gives us a vivid picture of "the day of the LORD"—the phrase used in Scripture for that final moment before the Lord returns in glory to judge the living and the dead.

If we want to understand the Book of Revelation, it is very helpful to trace the tradition of the Day of the Lord in Scripture and in the life of the people of God. Where did this idea come from? What had it come to signify by the time John wrote this book? And what does it mean for us today? These are just some of the questions we should explore before we plunge into Revelation itself.

Precursors and Prophecies

The Bible begins to speak of a Day of the Lord in the Book of Amos, which was written in the middle of the eighth century before Christ. The prophet calls the ladies of Samaria "cows of Bashan" (Amos 4:1) who oppress the poor, crush the needy, and call to their husbands to bring them something to drink. For them the Day of the Lord will be a day of unexpected disaster, "as when someone runs away from a lion only to meet a bear, goes into his house and puts his hand on the wall, only for a snake to bite him" (5:19). It will be a day of retribution for their selfishness and injustice.

Once this retribution has occurred in the form of the Babylonian Exile, the Day of the Lord becomes a day of hope, a day for the Lord to re-establish his chosen people in their beloved Jerusalem, a day of peace, serenity and justice, when "the wolf will live with the lamb, the lion eat hay like the ox" (Isaiah 11:6-7), and all nations come to "draw water from the springs of salvation" in Zion (12:3). This vision of joy becomes more and more vivid as various prophets come and go: The Lord "will rejoice over you with happy song, he will renew you by his love; he will dance with shouts of joy for you" (Zephaniah 3:17). The day will give birth to a new world, depicted in graphic terms of cosmic disturbances, when "the eternal mountains are dislodged; the everlasting hills sink down" (Habakkuk 3:6). All as the prophet cries, "Prepare in the desert a way for the LORD, make a straight highway for our God" (Isaiah 40:3).

During the years of Israel's misery and depression, these were encouraging words. The trouble was that this great day never seemed to come. The people were released from captivity in Babylon by Cyrus, but had to compete for a place in Jerusalem with the rabble that had filled the empty spaces. The Egyptians came from the south to trample over the land. The Syrians came from the north to try and stamp out the Jewish faith and way of life. The Romans came from the west and milked the country for taxes. There was no prophet to guide them, and even the Lord seemed to have deserted them. One group of Jews even abandoned Jerusalem and its sacred Temple, going out into the desert of Judea to await on the shores of the Dead Sea the messenger who would prepare a way for the Lord. In anticipation of his arrival, they would set a place for the messenger every evening at their communal dinner table.

The Day Is at Hand

But then a wild, prophetic figure appeared at the ford of the main road to the east across the Jordan. He gathered his followers into a community of repentance, symbolically washing them in the muddy waters of the Jordan as he heralded the imminent coming of the messenger. "Change your ways!" this new prophet shouted. "The sovereignty of God is upon you!"

This new prophet—John the Baptist—did not minister for long before he yielded leadership to a disciple of his, a man of magnetic personality who went around healing the sick, welcoming outcasts, and teaching authoritatively how to keep the divine law. This fellow even claimed the divine authority to forgive sin! "Are you the messenger of the Day of the Lord?" asked a puzzled John the Baptizer, only to be sent word that described his activities in the language of Isaiah's prophecies (Matthew 11:2; see Luke 7:22). When this new teacher—called Jesus of Nazareth—staged a demonstration in the Temple calling into question the whole tried system of Judaism, the hostile custodians of the Temple asked, "Who gave you authority to act like this?" (Matthew 21:23).

They soon got rid of Jesus and his intolerable claims, and the movement seemed to fizzle out like fireworks on a wet evening. But a motley group of his followers reappeared with the claim that his execution really had turned the world upside-down. God had raised him up, "seated him at his own right hand" (Psalm 110 said), made him "son of God in power," and given him (as Daniel put it) "all authority in heaven and on earth." They claimed, too, that Joel's prophecy had been fulfilled: "I shall pour out my spirit on all humanity. I shall show portents in the sky and signs on the earth" (Joel 2:28-30). But they didn't seem to be quite sure whether the old world had actually ended and a new state of the world begun, or whether it was merely still frighteningly imminent.

The Day of the Lord and the Kingdom of God

The coming of the kingdom had filled Jesus' whole horizon, from his first proclamation to the last words of his trial: "You will see the Son of Man coming on the clouds of heaven" (Mark 14:62). "My kingdom is not of this world" (John 18:36). Even the central petition of the Lord's Prayer, which Matthew places at the center of his Sermon on the Mount, is "Your kingdom come!" (Matthew 6:10). In the synoptic gospels, Jesus is so focused on the kingship of his Father that he barely tells us about himself. He is too busy proclaiming the "sovereignty" of God, the fact of God genuinely being accepted as undisputed ruler of all.

This sovereignty of God, presaged by Jesus in his miracles, was a kingdom of divine healing; an end to suffering, alienation, and fear; a joyful welcome for sinners into the divine peace, inspired by and validating the dreams of the prophets. It all sounds so pleasant, doesn't it? But this kingdom comes to its culmination in the perfect and willing obedience of Jesus in his self-offering. It comes in his brutal death—an act of obedience to God that rights the disobedience that humanity, or "Adam," displayed in Eden. Then God truly reigns over humanity.

What did Jesus and his followers believe would happen next? The only literature that they knew was the Bible, so they expressed their belief in the terms of the prophets and the psalms. The later books of the Old Testament and the literature that was contemporary to Jesus portrays the decisive intervention of God in terms of cosmic disturbances, and we find a similar portrayal in the gospels.

These statements can be disorienting and hard to follow, as the gospel writers move from a factual statement, "He breathed his last," to an imaged comment, ". . . and the veil of the Temple was torn in two" (Matthew 27:50, 51; Mark 15:37, 38). So how did the Day of the Lord manifest itself? Earthquakes at the crucifixion and resurrection? Skeletons rising from their tombs and clattering into Jerusalem? Stars falling from heaven? Even when we view these events in metaphorical terms, as Christians we must believe that the "hour" of Jesus (as the evangelist John calls his death and resurrection) was the Day of the Lord that the prophets had been speaking of for centuries.

The day had come, and it introduced a completely new state of affairs. Nothing would ever be the same again. All that remains now is for God's rule to reach completion. It is like the soft, pink light of African dawn that will change inevitably to blazing noontime brightness.

Our Own Resurrection

This is all well and good, but what's in it for us? The answer is not limited to the heavens falling around our ears. There is, of course, the fanfare of the last trumpet to announce the event, and the Lord's triumphal procession on the clouds (see 1 Thessalonians 4:16-17). But Paul also uses more personal and intimate language. He states repeatedly that we who are baptized into Christ's death begin even now to live a new life in Christ—and we will be raised up at the last day in a resurrection like his. While we await that final resurrection, we are called to live with Jesus' life—a life no longer our own. And this is what leads us to be transformed into him more and more. Grown into the risen Christ, we have joined the first-fruits from the dead. And when we are raised (both men and women) to sonship in him, we will fully enjoy his inheritance. When he hands over the kingdom to God the Father—and the last enemy to be done away with is death itself—so everyone who is in Christ will come to life.

If Jesus is the prime model of this transformed, "resurrection life," then what can we say our own resurrection will look like? What conclusions can we draw by looking at Jesus? It is interesting that the risen Christ was not immediately recognizable, even to his friends. He could enter a room though its doors were closed, but he could eat fish. He clearly has a physical body—no phantasm or ghost—but not like the physical bodies we know. Paul never says what sort of body it is, and even calls this a stupid question (see 1 Corinthians 15:35-36). He does, however, tell us a few things:

"What is sown is perishable, but what is raised is imperishable." No more loss of hair and teeth, no more decay. Instead, we take on the imperishability of God.

"What is sown is contemptible, but what is raised is glorious." No more fear or worry; everything that shames us is no longer shameful but is our glory, transformed into the blazing glory of God.

"What is sown is weak, but what is raised is powerful." No more failure or weakness ("I can't lift my suitcase." "I can't face this problem"). Rather, all our weakness is transformed into the gentle, firm, unlimited power of God.

"What is sown is soul, but what is raised is spirit." The life principle—what it is that makes us live and function—is no longer the human soul but is the Spirit of God.

The first three of these transformations are actually summed up in the fourth, and so Paul gives us all we need to know about our final personal destiny (see 1 Corinthians 15:42-44). What it feels like for me to have the Spirit of God as my life-principle, I cannot say. I will still be myself, but with none of my limitations or worries, fears or failures, for I will be enlarged, empowered, and comforted in the grasp of God.

Changed by His Glory

A kingdom, however, is not made up solely of individual persons, and in a field where we can talk only in images, all the imagery of what is to come is corporate and expansive: a new heaven and a new earth, the restoration of all things, the wedding feast of the Lamb, a new and glorious city coming down from heaven. Images speak for themselves and can never be wholly analyzed, but all these images speak of things returned to what they should be, or to a situation even better than anything experienced before: the happiest occasion with the most wonderful companions, everything fresh, unspoiled, unalloyed in joy, or, as the Eucharistic Prayer so touchingly puts it, "when every tear will be wiped away."

However these images represent it, the reality of the Day of the Lord is on a completely new plane, a plane that is not easy to describe. And that makes sense, really. After all, how could it be described in cold human terms when we have no experience of it? Still, overarching everything is the image of glory. This "glory" is not what we know as glory—congratulations, human acclaim, medals, and adulation. It is a specifically divine attribute that may only be glimpsed in this life. It is glittering, sparkling, likened to the bright sunlight. But even so, in the new city there will be no sun or lamplight, for the radiant glory of God and of the Lamb is the lighted torch.

When the blaze of God's glory is encountered in the revelations of the Old Testament, it inspires not only awe but also terror in the face of human inadequacy and sin. But there is no trace of that fear in John's writings: "We saw his glory, glory as of an only-begotten son from the Father" (John 1:14). In the heavenly court

(Revelation 4–5), while the angels cry, "Holy, holy, holy," the saints all cry, "Glory!" Perhaps this is the effect of perfect love that casts out fear, for the keynote of the new city of God is gold and light and glory—the glory that comes when his servants see him face to face (see Revelation 22:4).

The Kingdom Is Here!

We have been reflecting on what theologians call "eschatology," the doctrine of the last things. So what about the timing? From the time of Amos onward, this day has been spoken of; when will we see it? Actually, the Day of the Lord has come already in the "hour" of Jesus' death and resurrection. Its final consummation is in the future—which is why we rightly pray, "Your kingdom come!" But it is also true that the kingdom has already come in the crucifixion and glorification of Jesus.

That incomparable document of Vatican II on the Church, *Lumen Gentium*, devotes a whole chapter to the "Eschatological Nature of the Pilgrim Church and her Union with the Heavenly Church." In that chapter, the Council Fathers taught that we should no longer make a sharp division between the church militant and the church triumphant. The glorified Lord is continually active in the world, and the promised restoration has already begun. Even now the church is marked by a genuine though imperfect holiness. All who belong to Christ form one church, the wayfarers together with the brothers and sisters who sleep in the peace of Christ. We already can experience a vital fellowship with our brothers and sisters who are in heavenly glory.

This promise of present glory is manifested with particular strength in the tradition of the Eastern Churches, where the veneration of icons brings to mind the presence of the saints all around those who praise God. And above all, it is present in the Eucharist, where the saints join us in offering the unique sacrifice of Christ. As the Council Fathers wrote: "In the earthly liturgy we take part in a foretaste of that heavenly liturgy which is celebrated in the holy city of Jerusalem toward which we journey as pilgrims" (Decree on the Liturgy, *Sacrosanctum Concilium*, 8).

So as you move on to pray through the Book of Revelation, keep in mind the awesome promises that God has fulfilled in Christ. Remember that you too are a new creation in the Lord, and that you can begin to experience the joy and power of heaven right now. Every time you go to Mass, know that you are entering into the courts of the Lord. Believe that the whole host of heaven is with you, and join them in celebrating the long-awaited Day of the Lord. Together with all of them, sing with your whole heart:

> *Holy, holy, holy, Lord God of power and might!*
> *Heaven and earth are full of your glory!*

"The Revelation of Jesus Christ"

Revelation 1:1-20

"The Revelation of Jesus Christ"

"The Revelation of Jesus Christ"
Revelation 1:1-20

Revelation 1:1-6

¹ The revelation of Jesus Christ, which God gave him to show his servants what must soon take place; he made it known by sending his angel to his servant John, ²who testified to the word of God and to the testimony of Jesus Christ, even to all that he saw.

³ Blessed is the one who reads aloud the words of the prophecy, and blessed are those who hear and who keep what is written in it; for the time is near.

⁴ John to the seven churches that are in Asia:

Grace to you and peace from him who is and who was and who is to come, and from the seven spirits who are before his throne, ⁵and from Jesus Christ, the faithful witness, the firstborn of the dead, and the ruler of the kings of the earth.

To him who loves us and freed us from our sins by his blood, ⁶and made us to be a kingdom, priests serving his God and Father, to him be glory and dominion forever and ever. Amen.

Even people who haven't seen the *Star Wars* movies know that they are science fiction and not history. Well, the Book of Revelation is another example of a work that should be approached with a basic understanding of its style and purpose. The Book of Revelation is prophecy, not prediction.

Just as *Star Wars* doesn't really depict what happened "a long time ago in a galaxy far, far away," so Revelation doesn't depict exactly what will happen a long time from now, when heaven comes to earth. Rather, it represents a type of literature called "apocalyptic," which was especially popular from around 200 B.C. to A.D. 200.

Using symbolic images and language, the Book of Revelation is meant to point to truths about God's judgment at the end of human history and about what is needed for salvation.

What are the conditions for salvation? Above all, do not abandon your fervor and devotion for God, your "first love" (see Revelation 2:4). Think of the love between newlyweds. The effort to set up a household, adjust to one another's habits, and develop a new work schedule often occurs under difficult situations, yet "first love" causes the couple to remember these early times with humor and tenderness.

Don't we all know "religious" people who seem burdened and grim as they try to please God? Perhaps they have lost some of that first love that brings joy into even difficult tasks. Perhaps they need to make some adjustments in the way they live, in order to renew and nurture their love for God.

What about you? Are there moments when you can pause and allow Jesus' presence to fill your heart? It might be a reflective moment after Mass, or a brief moment of quiet that gives you a chance to rest in the Lord's loving embrace. Is there a sin that calls for repentance? Seek forgiveness, and know the energy that comes from a heart made light by Jesus' love. Be attentive to the Spirit, and come back to your first love!

"Lord of my salvation, perfect lover, gladden me with more of your love and presence. May I never forget that you are the source of life."

Revelation 1:7-11

7   Look! He is coming with the clouds;
        every eye will see him,
    even those who pierced him;

and on his account all the tribes
　　of the earth will wail.
So it is to be. Amen.
8 "I am the Alpha and the Omega," says the Lord God, who is and
who was and who is to come, the Almighty.
9 I, John, your brother who share with you in Jesus the persecution and the kingdom and the patient endurance, was on the island
called Patmos because of the word of God and the testimony of Jesus.
10I was in the spirit on the Lord's day, and I heard behind me a loud
voice like a trumpet 11saying, "Write in a book what you see and
send it to the seven churches, to Ephesus, to Smyrna, to Pergamum,
to Thyatira, to Sardis, to Philadelphia, and to Laodicea."

If you were to list the top three blessings you would want to ask
from the Lord, would one of those blessings be endurance? How
about fortitude or patience? We know we would need such gifts
if we were going to face suffering or trials. But it's not something we
like to think about. We'd rather ask for health, wealth, and happi-
ness. In other words, we'd rather avoid suffering than ask for the gifts
we need to face it gracefully.

But the truth is that no matter how hard we try to avoid them,
difficulties have a way of finding us. They are simply a part of life
on this earth. So rather than try to run away from the inevitable,
perhaps we would do better to ask what would bring us the most
hope, strength, and comfort when suffering does come our way.

John tells us that he is our brother in tribulation, and that he
shares in our patient endurance. Evidently, he has found a way to
deal with his own difficult life—a life of exile and deprivation on
the island of Patmos. So what was it that helped him? Nothing
more than the firm conviction that Jesus was going to come back!
Jesus Christ, the Alpha and Omega, the almighty and everlasting one, will be revealed to all the nations, even those who have

rejected him and his followers. No matter what he may face, John knows that this hope will never change.

Let's face it: daily life can be a grind. It's not hard to feel worn down by all of our responsibilities, overwhelmed by worries, or agitated by injustices. As a result, we can forget that our lives are enfolded in Christ. We are not alone, trudging through life's difficulties with no one to help us. We are in the midst of God's eternal plan. Jesus is with us, and his Holy Spirit is working in and through us! Because Christ really is coming again, our lives have a purpose and a goal beyond simply making it to the end of a day or completing all the items on our to-do list.

When you pray today, lift your eyes heavenward. Ask Jesus to give you a vision of the end, when his promises will be fulfilled and you will see him face to face. Imagine what it will be like when everyone sees him, and everything is put right. Let this heavenly vision inspire you and give you hope; let it strengthen you to endure patiently and even joyfully whatever may come your way today. After all, you know the end of the story!

"Jesus, let me never forget that you are coming back. Fill my heart today, so that the vision of your heavenly glory will lift me up and give me a new perspective. Come, Lord, and give me fortitude, patience, and joy!"

Revelation 1:12-20

[12] Then I turned to see whose voice it was that spoke to me, and on turning I saw seven golden lampstands, [13]and in the midst of the lampstands I saw one like the Son of Man, clothed with a long robe and with a golden sash across his chest. [14]His head and his hair were white as white wool, white as snow; his eyes were like a flame of fire, [15]his feet were like burnished bronze, refined as in a furnace, and his

voice was like the sound of many waters. [16]In his right hand he held seven stars, and from his mouth came a sharp, two-edged sword, and his face was like the sun shining with full force.

[17] When I saw him, I fell at his feet as though dead. But he placed his right hand on me, saying, "Do not be afraid; I am the first and the last, [18]and the living one. I was dead, and see, I am alive forever and ever; and I have the keys of Death and of Hades. [19]Now write what you have seen, what is, and what is to take place after this. [20]As for the mystery of the seven stars that you saw in my right hand, and the seven golden lampstands: the seven stars are the angels of the seven churches, and the seven lampstands are the seven churches.

One of the goals of apocalyptic writings like the Book of Revelation is to encourage believers in times of trial. But sometimes it can be hard to understand how we are to be encouraged by the bizarre or even frightening images painted by John in this book: a dragon with seven heads, a beast rising out of the sea, the sun disappearing while the moon turns to blood. Likewise, it can be intimidating to imagine Jesus with burning eyes, a voice like the ocean, and a sword coming from his mouth. This is not your typical shepherd carrying a little lost lamb on his shoulders!

It's important, as we read this passage, to remember that this description of Jesus is not intended to be a portrait of him, as one might think about the *Mona Lisa* or a photograph of the president. This description is meant to paint a word picture of various attributes of Christ—attributes that we would do well to remember when we face difficulties or confusion.

It's also helpful to know that the imagery that John used to describe Jesus in this passage was well known by the readers of his time. Much of it, in fact, bore striking similarities to popular writings from the Hebrew Bible: the Book of Daniel, for instance, and 1 and 2 Maccabees. These images are meant to evoke Jesus' power, authority, and divinity. They are meant to communicate his greatness, so that those who have given their lives to him will know that he is with them and will protect them.

The encouraging point for us is that John sees Jesus in all his power and glory—and we can see him as well! In our prayer, when we go to Mass, or when we read the Scriptures, we can go beyond the mental exercise of affirming our faith in Jesus' victory. When we turn to him, he will reveal himself to us and fill our hearts as well as our minds.

What will we see? Maybe we will experience the sword of his word exposing and cutting away our sin. Maybe we will feel the piercing gaze of his look of love. Perhaps we will hear his voice calling us with the strength of the ocean. We might be impressed by his purity and his desire to make us pure as well. Perhaps we will be overwhelmed by his kingly authority over our every anxiety. Jesus knows what we need in each particular moment of our lives, and he is eager to reveal himself to us and care for us.

When you pray today, expect Jesus to show himself to you. He wants you to know him. He wants you to take strength in the fact that he who is all powerful is standing with you no matter what you may be going through.

"Jesus, I turn toward you to gaze on your beauty and your glory. Reveal yourself to me, Lord, so that I will come to know you and love you with all my heart."

Seven Letters to Seven Churches

Revelation 2:1–3:22

Seven Letters to Seven Churches
Revelation 2:1–3:22

Revelation 2:1-7

[1] "To the angel of the church in Ephesus write: These are the words of him who holds the seven stars in his right hand, who walks among the seven golden lampstands:
[2] "I know your works, your toil and your patient endurance. I know that you cannot tolerate evildoers; you have tested those who claim to be apostles but are not, and have found them to be false. [3]I also know that you are enduring patiently and bearing up for the sake of my name, and that you have not grown weary. [4]But I have this against you, that you have abandoned the love you had at first. [5]Remember then from what you have fallen; repent, and do the works you did at first. If not, I will come to you and remove your lampstand from its place, unless you repent. [6]Yet this is to your credit: you hate the works of the Nicolaitans, which I also hate. [7]Let anyone who has an ear listen to what the Spirit is saying to the churches. To everyone who conquers, I will give permission to eat from the tree of life that is in the paradise of God."

How have we responded to God's grace in our lives? In the gospels, we see many reactions to Jesus. Some were openly hostile, some colored by the person's total absorption in worldly affairs. Some were free and generous toward Jesus. The rich man wanted to follow Jesus but was attached to his earthly goods (Matthew 19:16-22); Martha tended to be legalistic, but Mary gave her whole heart to Jesus (John 12:3-8). The introduction to Revelation exhorts us to listen closely to God's words and respond to them (see Revelation 1:3).

The Christians in Ephesus had many commendable qualities. Their works, toil, and patient endurance (Revelation 2:2) were fine characteristics and reflected a strong faith that enabled them to stand firm in their Christian commitment (2:3). Their wisdom and discernment in defending the true faith against false teachers was especially laudable (2:2).

Despite these good qualities, God was displeased with the Ephesians because they had lost the love and enthusiasm they had had at the time of their conversion (Revelation 2:5). God was calling them to return to the fervor of their earlier days and to allow this joy to permeate their lives. Too often, we discount the value of an enthusiastic response to the Lord and settle for more comfortable but inactive Christian lives.

When God's truths are clear in our minds and his love penetrates our hearts, we can't help but respond in a joyful way. The enthusiasm God wants is not just reflected in a shallow emotionalism, an outgoing personality, or an eagerness to serve. It comes from an interior abiding in God's presence, which leads one to a deep love for God *and* humanity.

Some signs of an authentic response are a longing to be in God's presence at the liturgy and through personal prayer and Scripture reading. It is reflected in our desire to be in communion with the whole church and in our love for others, in our desire to share the gospel with others and to serve the suffering, poor, and lonely, just as Jesus did. It is revealed in our trust in God and in our willingness to submit our lives to the work of the blood and the cross of Christ in any situation. Such traits are pleasing to God because they reflect a love and enthusiasm for him that is consistent with our God-given personalities and talents.

"Father, may I eagerly embrace Jesus' work on the cross and wholeheartedly live the fullness of his resurrection life."

Revelation 2:8-11

8 "And to the angel of the church in Smyrna write: These are the words of the first and the last, who was dead and came to life: 9 "I know your affliction and your poverty, even though you are rich. I know the slander on the part of those who say that they are Jews and are not, but are a synagogue of Satan. 10Do not fear what you are about to suffer. Beware, the devil is about to throw some of you into prison so that you may be tested, and for ten days you will have affliction. Be faithful until death, and I will give you the crown of life. 11Let anyone who has an ear listen to what the Spirit is saying to the churches. Whoever conquers will not be harmed by the second death."

These are the words of the first and the last, who was dead and came to life. (Revelation 2:8)

As you read the letters to the churches from the Book of Revelation, notice the way Jesus describes himself at the outset of each letter. It will give you a clue to the theme of the letter—what the church needs to understand in order to achieve ultimate victory in its struggles.

To the church at Smyrna, Jesus describes himself as the one who died and came to life, the resurrected one. He understood the hardships they faced; but, instead of telling them he would spare them, he told them not to be afraid! Why? Because he himself was dead and now is alive. He did it; he passed through suffering and death, and now he promises that he will take the church at Smyrna through as well. Jesus' resurrection proves that there is life on the other side, and his love proves that we can be there with him!

Here's a question worth pondering: does my faith in the resurrection have an impact on my everyday life? We may not be called upon to die or go to prison for our faith. Still, every day we face different kinds of "death." There is a kind of death involved when we face the choice of holding on to or letting go of a comfort in our life that tends to weaken our faith or lead us into temptation. There is also the death that comes when physical illness takes away not only our health but our confidence or independence as well. Sometimes it is an external circumstance that calls us to let go. Imagine a father who loses his job in December and won't have money to buy Christmas gifts for his family. It might be a smaller yet still difficult setback, like a last-minute cancellation of a vacation or a family visit.

Whenever we face the stripping away of such things, is our response fear or anger? Jesus understands. Remember, he has walked the path before us and calls us to let him walk with us now. He longs to lead us through difficulties, great or small, into the life on the other side. As we hold fast to him and allow him to bring life out of these little deaths, we will find our confidence in him erasing our fears. Our faith in his resurrection, put into practice in this way, will prepare us for eternal life with him. Like the victorious in Smyrna, we will "not be harmed by the second death" (Revelation 2:11).

"Lord, in your humanity, you have passed through suffering and death. Let me not feel abandoned when I face the same. Instead, help me to grasp your hand and walk with you into the life on the other side!"

Revelation 2:12-17

[12] "And to the angel of the church in Pergamum write: These are the words of him who has the sharp two-edged sword:
[13] "I know where you are living, where Satan's throne is. Yet you are holding fast to my name, and you did not deny your faith in me even

in the days of Antipas my witness, my faithful one, who was killed among you, where Satan lives. [14]But I have a few things against you: you have some there who hold to the teaching of Balaam, who taught Balak to put a stumbling block before the people of Israel, so that they would eat food sacrificed to idols and practice fornication. [15]So you also have some who hold to the teaching of the Nicolaitans. [16]Repent then. If not, I will come to you soon and make war against them with the sword of my mouth. [17]Let anyone who has an ear listen to what the Spirit is saying to the churches. To everyone who conquers I will give some of the hidden manna, and I will give a white stone, and on the white stone is written a new name that no one knows except the one who receives it."

I t's not really a lie—I just didn't tell the whole the truth." "I have no problem reading horoscopes with my friends—I don't really believe in them." "There's no problem leafing through a provocative magazine—it's just like looking at a menu. I'm not going to order anything." Every day we are faced with opportunities to compromise our Christian faith. It may not seem like such a big deal, because we're not overtly denying Jesus. But the consequences can be greater than we imagine.

The church in Pergamum had similar problems. A famous city, it was the home of a great temple to Caesar that was the heart of emperor worship at the time. This is why John calls it "Satan's throne." In fact, it was a place of great political power, where the governor regularly heard legal cases. The people of Pergamum had plenty of complicated choices. Should they go to a nonbeliever's banquet, when some of the food might have been sacrificed to idols? What about buying meat at the market, where it was hard to know whether it had come from the pagan temple? Their temptation was to "bend the rules" a little bit so that they could fit into the rest of society.

The dilemma confronting the believers in Pergamum is the same that we face today: the limits of cultural assimilation. It is tempting to try to find "loopholes" in our faith to justify becoming one of the crowd; we can excuse our behavior on a moral technicality, or try to put a positive spin on our actions, but in the end, we still have to ask whether we are compromising our faith in order to reap the passing benefits of the world.

Jesus appeared to Pergamum with a sharp, two-edged sword, to cut through the subtle deceptions of the devil. He knows that Satan's primary strategy is to chip away at our faith little by little so that over time he can separate us from Christ without our even recognizing it. But Jesus promises that when we make right choices, rejecting temptation and focusing our hearts on the outward riches offered by the world, we will receive heavenly riches instead—the hidden manna and the stone with a new name. We will be satisfied deeply by Christ; we will have dignity as God's sons and daughters, something that those immersed in the world simply can't understand.

"Jesus, bring your sword to cut away the subtle compromises that tie me to the empty riches of this world. I want to be satisfied and nourished by you, even if the world can't recognize my success."

Revelation 2:18-29

[18] "And to the angel of the church in Thyatira write: These are the words of the Son of God, who has eyes like a flame of fire, and whose feet are like burnished bronze:
[19] "I know your works—your love, faith, service, and patient endurance. I know that your last works are greater than the first. [20]But I have this against you: you tolerate that woman Jezebel, who calls herself a prophet and is teaching and beguiling my servants to prac-

tice fornication and to eat food sacrificed to idols. [21]I gave her time to repent, but she refuses to repent of her fornication. [22]Beware, I am throwing her on a bed, and those who commit adultery with her I am throwing into great distress, unless they repent of her doings; [23]and I will strike her children dead. And all the churches will know that I am the one who searches minds and hearts, and I will give to each of you as your works deserve. [24]But to the rest of you in Thyatira, who do not hold this teaching, who have not learned what some call 'the deep things of Satan,' to you I say, I do not lay on you any other burden; [25]only hold fast to what you have until I come. [26]To everyone who conquers and continues to do my works to the end,

I will give authority over the nations;
[27] to rule them with an iron rod,
        as when clay pots are shattered—
[28]even as I also received authority from my Father. To the one who conquers I will also give the morning star. [29]Let anyone who has an ear listen to what the Spirit is saying to the churches."

The church in Thyatira seemed to be doing well; its members demonstrated the sought-after virtues of love and faith, service, and patient endurance. They were unwavering—in fact, increasing—in their work for God and his kingdom. So what did Jesus have against them? The problem was that the church did nothing to stop a false teacher who was leading the people into idolatry. The false prophet was referred to as "Jezebel"—a name that hearkened back to the pagan wife of Old Testament king Ahab, who convinced him to worship idols. The "deep things of Satan" probably referred to so-called hidden knowledge of events surrounding the end of the world.

Obviously, despite the virtues of the people of Thyatira, some of the people in the church there were getting sidetracked and going along with teachings that were contrary to the gospel. It was not enough for them to rest on their accomplishments; "holding fast" to what they had would involve challenging the sin in their midst.

It's not hard to understand the dilemma. At times, we can be so concerned with our personal lives, trying to grow in holiness or working for the Lord, that we overlook what would otherwise be obvious sins. We may be trying to advance in one area of our faith, while at the same time we ignore problems in another area. For instance, we may be so focused on our own growth in holiness that we forget the fact that we are part of the body of Christ and that Jesus is calling us to help the church as a whole to move forward. Caught up in our private lives of faith, we may have become deaf to the cry of the poor or the call to justice in our community.

When you see a family member getting involved in something that is harmful, do you turn away, or do you storm heaven in inter-cession and look for opportunities to win that person over to Christ? Do you allow gossip or cheating to take place at work, as long as you don't participate in it? Or do you try to say something or look for peaceful ways to offer alternatives? In your own life, do you focus on having a good prayer time, and yet tolerate "little white lies"? Let's not put blinders on when it comes to living our faith. Let's hold fast to what Jesus has done, and not tolerate anything in ourselves or our loved ones that distorts the gospel!

"Jesus, gaze on me with your eyes, like a flame of fire. Pierce through my individualism and through any hollow reliance I have on my own holy actions. Help me not to tolerate sin, but hold fast to what you have given me."

Revelation 3:1-6

[1] "And to the angel of the church in Sardis write: These are the words of him who has the seven spirits of God and the seven stars:

"I know your works; you have a name of being alive, but you are dead. ²Wake up, and strengthen what remains and is on the point of death, for I have not found your works perfect in the sight of my God. ³Remember then what you received and heard; obey it, and repent. If you do not wake up, I will come like a thief, and you will not know at what hour I will come to you. ⁴Yet you have still a few persons in Sardis who have not soiled their clothes; they will walk with me, dressed in white, for they are worthy. ⁵If you conquer, you will be clothed like them in white robes, and I will not blot your name out of the book of life; I will confess your name before my Father and before his angels. ⁶Let anyone who has an ear listen to what the Spirit is saying to the churches."

I have not found your works perfect in the sight of my God.
(Revelation 3:2)

Is this letter for real? Did Jesus really want the members of the church in Sardis to produce nothing but "perfect works"? If that's the case, then maybe it's true that very few people indeed will make it to heaven. After all, who among us can confess to having done everything perfectly?

Perhaps we would do well to examine what it means to be perfect—at least according to the Scriptures. We're all pretty familiar with a modern-day definition of perfection: absolute freedom from any error, complete purity, and flawlessness in every way. The superlatives flow without ceasing, each one convicting us more and more of our own imperfection. But this isn't really how the Scriptures define perfection—or at least not how Jesus defines it. In one of the most often-quoted passages from the gospels, he does tell us to be perfect as our heavenly Father is perfect (Matthew 5:48). Yes, that does sound just as intimidating—and unattainable—as the other definitions described above. But that is simply the way

Matthew's Gospel presents Jesus' command. If we look at Luke, we find another dimension of Jesus' teaching that gives us a broader perspective—one that helps balance out the sense of complete flawlessness. As Luke describes it, Jesus told us to be merciful as our heavenly Father is merciful (Luke 6:36).

Another passage—this one from St. Paul—gives us yet another way of looking at perfection. In his famous "sermon on love" in 1 Corinthians 13, Paul tells us about what life will be like at the end of time, when Jesus comes back: "When the complete comes, the partial will come to an end" (13:10). In this passage, the word for "complete" is the same word that Matthew used when he talked about being "perfect," and that John used in the passage above from Revelation. Perfection, in this sense, has more to do with the completion of a plan and intention than it does with any lack of error or mistake. Something is "perfect" when it has finally fulfilled the task for which it was intended.So if we put these together, what can we conclude about the "perfect works" that the church in Sardis was lacking in? For one, it seems that they may have been tempted to give up on the calling they had received to follow Jesus to the best of their abilities: their faith—and the obedience of their faith—was lacking because they had lost sight of who they were and what Jesus had empowered them to do. And perhaps their works were "imperfect" because they had lost sight of the mercy that they had "received and heard" from the Lord, and so were reluctant in showing one another the same kind of mercy.

Brothers and sisters, this is our calling as well: not to be completely flawless in everything we do but to open our hearts to all the mercy Jesus has given to us and to remain as committed as possible to showing that mercy to everyone we know. We don't have to get it right all the time. We just have to keep trying our best and ask the Holy Spirit to pick us up whenever we fall.

"Jesus, I want to be just as perfect—as merciful—as your Father is. Please flood my heart with your own perfect mercy, so that I can shower the world with it as well. Come, Lord, and make me like you!"

Revelation 3:7-13

7 "And to the angel of the church in Philadelphia write:
These are the words of the holy one, the true one,
who has the key of David,
who opens and no one will shut,
who shuts and no one opens:
8 "I know your works. Look, I have set before you an open door, which no one is able to shut. I know that you have but little power, and yet you have kept my word and have not denied my name. 9I will make those of the synagogue of Satan who say that they are Jews and are not, but are lying—I will make them come and bow down before your feet, and they will learn that I have loved you. 10Because you have kept my word of patient endurance, I will keep you from the hour of trial that is coming on the whole world to test the inhabitants of the earth. 11I am coming soon; hold fast to what you have, so that no one may seize your crown. 12If you conquer, I will make you a pillar in the temple of my God; you will never go out of it. I will write on you the name of my God, and the name of the city of my God, the new Jerusalem that comes down from my God out of heaven, and my own new name. 13Let anyone who has an ear listen to what the Spirit is saying to the churches."

Look, I have set before you an open door, which no one is able to shut.
(Revelation 3:8)

What a message of hope! Jesus has opened the door for us, and *it cannot be shut*. Oh, how often it seems that the door is shut when we face challenges to our faith! We may think that heaven itself has closed its doors to us, perhaps because of some hidden sin in our lives or because Jesus has deemed us unworthy of his grace and favor. Our weaknesses and limitations may seem so great that they block the way. But this is not the way Jesus works. He has opened the door, and no force in heaven or on earth can shut it to us.

Of course, it's up to us to walk through that door. And such a decision may involve repenting for whatever obstacles we ourselves may have set up. But even in this situation, the news is encouraging: it is never too late to turn away from sin and enter that door into eternal life. The door is always open, after all. We can go through it at any moment. When we persevere in hardship, that perseverance is pleasing to God and brings us to the entrance of the door. When we endure—even with the little strength we have—and do not deny Jesus, the door is before us. When we hold fast to Jesus, we are brought through the door!

And what happens when we pass through that door? We enter into the very temple of God in the new Jerusalem in heaven! We are given the crown of life, and we are marked with the name of Jesus, our victorious Lord. We become part of the heavenly landscape, never to be separated again from Jesus.

Even our enemies, even those who have persecuted us and maligned us, can enter. Imagine the joy we will experience if our own perseverance wins over someone who has opposed us! Imagine the joy we will experience if someone who has opposed God himself is moved to repentance because he or she has caught a glimpse of the love of God because of our witness! What better fruit of our perseverance than to bring about a change of heart in someone who has turned away from him?

Today is a good day to tell the Lord that you want to walk through that door with him. It's also a good day to tell him that you want to bring with you everyone who has caused you suffering, so that your witness of perseverance can add to the riches of his heavenly temple. May we all hold fast to Jesus and endure with patience whatever comes our way!

"Thank you, Lord, that you have opened the door of heaven to me. May many pass through that door to enjoy eternal life with you."

Revelation 3:14-22

14 "And to the angel of the church in Laodicea write: The words of the Amen, the faithful and true witness, the origin of God's creation: 15 "I know your works; you are neither cold nor hot. I wish that you were either cold or hot. 16So, because you are lukewarm, and neither cold nor hot, I am about to spit you out of my mouth. 17For you say, 'I am rich, I have prospered, and I need nothing.' You do not realize that you are wretched, pitiable, poor, blind, and naked. 18Therefore I counsel you to buy from me gold refined by fire so that you may be rich; and white robes to clothe you and to keep the shame of your nakedness from being seen; and salve to anoint your eyes so that you may see. 19I reprove and discipline those whom I love. Be earnest, therefore, and repent. 20Listen! I am standing at the door, knocking; if you hear my voice and open the door, I will come in to you and eat with you, and you with me. 21To the one who conquers I will give a place with me on my throne, just as I myself conquered and sat down with my Father on his throne. 22Let anyone who has an ear listen to what the Spirit is saying to the churches."

You do not realize that you are wretched, pitiable, poor, blind, and naked. (Revelation 3:17)

Situated as it was on an important trade route, the city of Laodicea profited from the business and industry that kept the Roman Empire humming along. Laodicea was also known for its textile businesses, especially for the fabrics it produced for upscale clothiers. Moreover, the city boasted a well-respected medical community, specializing in research that produced herbal salves for people's eyes. It's no wonder, then, that John's letter to the Christians in Laodicea used images of clothing and optical ointments to exhort the believers to turn back to the Lord. But why did he write such harsh words to them?

In an era when self-esteem has been raised to the level of an inalienable right, this brief letter can sound positively cruel. Surely there's nothing wrong with recounting the good elements of our lives. Can it be possible that Jesus wants us to focus our attention on everything that's *wrong* with us instead of recalling our blessings? Not really. As with everything else in the Christian life, it's a matter of balance, of both/and, not either/or.

The problem with the Laodiceans was not that they thought so highly of themselves for Jesus' tastes. Rather, it's that they had become so enamored of their professional successes that they let their prosperity lead them away from the Lord instead of closer to him in gratitude and love.

The truth is, God loves it when we put our talents to good use. He rejoices when we take advantage of the opportunities that life has given us. All we have to do is remember Jesus' parable of the talents, where a wealthy man rewards his industrious servants but is merciless toward the one who wasn't willing to take any risks (see Matthew 25:14-30). Clearly, God wants us to develop our gifts and make the most of our lives. He wants to see us succeed. The problem comes when we believe that we are the sole source of our success. The problem comes when we forget that everything we have comes from a loving, generous God whose gifts are meant to draw us closer to him and to move us to work for the common good (see 1 Corinthians 4:7; James 1:17).

How easy it is to find contentment in what we have accomplished! How tempting to love the gifts more than the giver—to let the fire of God's love grow lukewarm in our hearts as we spend all our time and attention on ourselves and our accomplishments! But how much more fulfillment can come when we develop our gifts for the sake of the Lord and his kingdom. How much more sense of purpose and usefulness is ours when we devote ourselves to building up other people and not just ourselves.

Brothers and sisters, Jesus has given us so much. Let's give it back to him—with interest! Let's not hold on to our gifts for ourselves but imitate the Lord by pouring our lives out for his people. Then, we will know a communion with Jesus that will far surpass anything this world has to offer.

"Jesus, I confess that without your generosity I too would be poor, pitiable, blind, and naked. But you have lavished your gifts upon me. In gratitude and love, I want to give it all back to you. I want to be your instrument in this world. Come, Lord, and use me for your glory!"

The Heavenly Court and Seven Seals

Revelation 4:1–8:5

The Heavenly Court and Seven Seals
Revelation 4:1–8:5

Revelation 4:1-11

[1] After this I looked, and there in heaven a door stood open! And the first voice, which I had heard speaking to me like a trumpet, said, "Come up here, and I will show you what must take place after this." [2]At once I was in the spirit, and there in heaven stood a throne, with one seated on the throne! [3]And the one seated there looks like jasper and carnelian, and around the throne is a rainbow that looks like an emerald. [4]Around the throne are twenty-four thrones, and seated on the thrones are twenty-four elders, dressed in white robes, with golden crowns on their heads. [5]Coming from the throne are flashes of lightning, and rumblings and peals of thunder, and in front of the throne burn seven flaming torches, which are the seven spirits of God; [6]and in front of the throne there is something like a sea of glass, like crystal.

Around the throne, and on each side of the throne, are four living creatures, full of eyes in front and behind: [7]the first living creature like a lion, the second living creature like an ox, the third living creature with a face like a human face, and the fourth living creature like a flying eagle. [8]And the four living creatures, each of them with six wings, are full of eyes all around and inside. Day and night without ceasing they sing,

"Holy, holy, holy,
the Lord God the Almighty,
who was and is and is to come."

[9] And whenever the living creatures give glory and honor and thanks to the one who is seated on the throne, who lives forever and ever, [10]the twenty-four elders fall before the one who is seated on the throne and worship the one who lives forever and ever; they

cast their crowns before the throne, singing,
¹¹ "You are worthy, our Lord and God,
>   to receive glory and honor and power,
> for you created all things,
>   and by your will they existed and were created."

After this I looked, and there in heaven a door stood open!
(Revelation 4:1)

The imagination is a wonderful tool God has given us. With it, we can envision possible paths we might take in our lives. When faced with a challenging task, we use our imaginations to plan how we will proceed. Our imaginations are also vital for our sense of play—from the games of "make believe" we played as little children to the complex puzzles and mind-teasers we delight in solving as adults.

Did you ever think about how your imagination can help you in prayer?

The fourth chapter of Revelation gives us a great opportunity to experiment with our imaginations. As you pray, close your eyes and picture the scene described here. Imagine yourself looking through an open door that leads to the throne of God. The light of God is illuminating everything brilliantly. Everything is made of precious jewels and costly fabrics. The beauty is overwhelming. Picture the angels and saints surrounding the throne with voices raised in majestic praise.

As you enter into God's throne room, imagine yourself joining in the heavenly praise and worship. Recount God's attributes one by one and praise him for each of them. Praise him for his beauty and glory, for his justice and holiness, for his love and compassion. Praise him for every aspect of his creation, as well. Recount the blessings he has given you and your family and praise him for each one. Given all of eternity, we will not exhaust the reasons to praise him.

When you pray today, be sure to use your natural gift of imagination to aid you. Praying like this has the power to lift us from a limited, natural set of expectations into an encounter with God on a spiritual plane that can transform our hearts and fill us with peace. The twenty-four elders laid their crowns before the Lord. Our crowns are our opinions, our talents, our ideas, our plans, and our achievements. Place these before his throne, and ask him to fill you with divine life instead. Let God reveal his mind to you. As you do, your heart will soften, and God's love will begin to move in you.

"Lord, you live in glorious light. Holy is your name. All praise and thanksgiving belong to you, O Lord! We bow down before you, for you are worthy."

Revelation 5:1-10

[1] Then I saw in the right hand of the one seated on the throne a scroll written on the inside and on the back, sealed with seven seals; [2]and I saw a mighty angel proclaiming with a loud voice, "Who is worthy to open the scroll and break its seals?" [3]And no one in heaven or on earth or under the earth was able to open the scroll or to look into it. [4]And I began to weep bitterly because no one was found worthy to open the scroll or to look into it. [5]Then one of the elders said to me, "Do not weep. See, the Lion of the tribe of Judah, the Root of David, has conquered, so that he can open the scroll and its seven seals."

[6] Then I saw between the throne and the four living creatures and among the elders a Lamb standing as if it had been slaughtered, having seven horns and seven eyes, which are the seven spirits of God

sent out into all the earth. ⁷He went and took the scroll from the right hand of the one who was seated on the throne. ⁸When he had taken the scroll, the four living creatures and the twenty-four elders fell before the Lamb, each holding a harp and golden bowls full of incense, which are the prayers of the saints. ⁹They sing a new song:

"You are worthy to take the scroll
and to open its seals,
for you were slaughtered and by
your blood you ransomed for God
saints from every tribe and
language and people and nation;
¹⁰ you have made them to be a kingdom and priests
serving our God,
and they will reign on earth."

John was writing to first-century Christians who were suffering greatly under persecution. Many had lost all their possessions and were being threatened with death if they did not renounce the Lord. The evil that confronted them seemed so vast that they undoubtedly were tempted to think that darkness would prevail.

We too can be tempted in this way when we are immersed in suffering—whether it be because of disease, life's problems, moral failures, or the sinful state of our society. John may have written to strengthen and encourage the Christians of his age, but his words can speak to us also, giving us a firm foundation for our security and assurance. God is on our side. Jesus has triumphed over evil. He now reigns over an everlasting kingdom. The Lamb, who was slain for our salvation, lives and is enthroned victorious in heaven.

In his vision, John saw God holding in his right hand a scroll that contained his purposes and counsels concerning the world. What are his purposes? That all peoples would be ransomed from sin and become a royal priesthood with direct access to this throne. And who is worthy to open this scroll and unlock the plans of God? Only one person is worthy—Jesus Christ. He was crucified for our sake, and through the shedding of his blood, he not only ransomed all peoples for God, he made them into saints serving God.

Such a vision—and the truths that such a vision reveals—can give us great comfort and security. Every one of God's intentions toward us is for good, not for evil. Every thought he has for us has to do with our blessing, our prosperity, and our growth in his holiness. At one time, it looked as if no one could open the scroll of God's plan and see it through to completion. But now, in Christ Jesus, we are secure. In him, every grace and blessing is available to us. We can surrender ourselves into his hands and obey him, knowing that he will never abandon us or betray us.

"Lord, I surrender myself into your hands. Cover me and all my family with your infinite love, mercy, grace, and power. Father, may your kingdom come and your will be done in my heart and throughout the earth."

Revelation 5:11-14

[11] Then I looked, and I heard the voice of many angels surrounding the throne and the living creatures and the elders; they numbered myriads of myriads and thousands of thousands, [12]singing with full voice,

"Worthy is the Lamb that was slaughtered
to receive power and wealth and wisdom and might
and honor and glory and blessing!"

[13]Then I heard every creature in heaven and on earth and under the earth and in the sea, and all that is in them, singing,

"To the one seated on the throne and to the Lamb
be blessing and honor and glory and might
forever and ever!"
[14]And the four living creatures said, "Amen!" And the elders fell
down and worshiped. ✺

Blessing and honor and glory and might forever and ever!
(Revelation 5:13)

What do you think about when you come to Mass, or engage
in personal prayer? Is your mind filled with the many needs
you have? Or, perhaps, with your concerns for the people
you love? Do you sometimes wonder whether your prayers make any
difference at all? After all, heaven is so big, and so many people have
even greater needs than you. Why would Jesus bother to hear your
voice?

Well, how about taking a different approach? How about seeing you prayer as joining a vast, never-ending chorus of worship to
God that has been rising since the very first moment of creation?
This is not just an exercise in imagination. Your voice really does
blend with multitudes of angels, throngs of holy men and women
of the past, every living creature, and even the forces of nature to
give God the glory he deserves. How's that for putting a different
perspective on the time you give to God each day?

The Book of Revelation gives us many glimpses into heavenly
worship, and these glimpses can really help our imagination when
we pray—especially on those days when the heavenly realities seem
distant to us. Try to picture heaven when you pray. Use your imagination. Surrounding God's throne are not just the "living creatures
and the elders" but voices of myriads of angels loudly proclaiming
the worthiness of the Lamb of God! Don't stop there. Imagine the
voices of "every creature in heaven and on earth and under the

earth and in the sea" raising their voices in praise to God and to the Lamb. And picture yourself right there in the middle of it all, thrilling to the sights and sounds even as you add to them with your own words of gratitude, love, praise, and petition.

When we come to God in prayer, no matter how feeble we feel our faith is, we join that heavenly chorus. God's greatness, Jesus' worthiness in itself, calls forth from all of creation proclamations of praise. We can praise him for his purity, for his humility, for his glory, for his power, for his victory, for his love. Any one of his attributes is enough inspiration for the heavenly chorus!

So ask God to open your eyes to the heavenly environment of worship—an environment that you can tap into every day. Let your voice enter into these songs of praise. Don't think that your prayer is weak or useless. Turn to the Lord in worship. Your heart will soar, and your needs will be met. Jesus is faithful!

"Almighty God, seated on the throne, you are worthy of all praise! Lamb of God who was slain, you deserve all glory and honor! May everything that has breath join in praising you forever and ever!"

Revelation 6:1-11

¹ Then I saw the Lamb open one of the seven seals, and I heard one of the four living creatures call out, as with a voice of thunder, "Come!" ²I looked, and there was a white horse! Its rider had a bow; a crown was given to him, and he came out conquering and to conquer.

³ When he opened the second seal, I heard the second living creature call out, "Come!" ⁴And out came another horse, bright red; its rider was permitted to take peace from the earth, so that people would slaughter one another; and he was given a great sword.

⁵ When he opened the third seal, I heard the third living creature

call out, "Come!" I looked, and there was a black horse! Its rider held a pair of scales in his hand, [6]and I heard what seemed to be a voice in the midst of the four living creatures saying, "A quart of wheat for a day's pay, and three quarts of barley for a day's pay, but do not damage the olive oil and the wine!"

[7] When he opened the fourth seal, I heard the voice of the fourth living creature call out, "Come!" [8]I looked and there was a pale green horse! Its rider's name was Death, and Hades followed with him; they were given authority over a fourth of the earth, to kill with sword, famine, and pestilence, and by the wild animals of the earth.

[9] When he opened the fifth seal, I saw under the altar the souls of those who had been slaughtered for the word of God and for the testimony they had given; [10]they cried out with a loud voice, "Sovereign Lord, holy and true, how long will it be before you judge and avenge our blood on the inhabitants of the earth?" [11]They were each given a white robe and told to rest a little longer, until the number would be complete both of their fellow servants and of their brothers and sisters, who were soon to be killed as they themselves had been killed.

Biblical scholars don't agree on whether John intended the four horsemen associated with the first four seals to represent historical events that had already occurred or some future events that had yet to be revealed. The conquest, war, economic upheaval, plague, and death described by them are graphic images of the fallout of conflict among nations, but it is not clear which nations they are referring to, or when all of this will occur. One thing is clear: since we are human beings living in a world affected by original sin, we can't avoid suffering the effects of such conflict—past, present, or future.

Throughout our history and into our foreseeable future, the world has been and will be racked by various forms of suffering brought about by conflict. What's more, this conflict has its otherworldly counterpart in the spiritual struggle of Satan against God. Like the saints of old, and like the martyrs described at the opening of the fifth seal, we can cry out, "How long, O Lord?" Even when we ourselves do not experience the effects of war or other conflicts, it pains us to see innocent people suffer and die needlessly. When will God show his justice? When will he put an end to this suffering?

When God tells the martyrs in Revelation that they must wait a little while, until the number of innocent deaths is complete, he is not being cruel. In fact, his response is a cause for hope because the very fact that a limit is placed on the number of martyrs means that the suffering will not go on forever. There will be a point at which it is over, when God's justice will finally be manifest to the whole of creation and when every tear will be wiped away.

We all need a little bit of this hope. It can be awfully discouraging to look at the state of the world. We may wonder why God doesn't just intervene right now and set everything right. So many of our brothers and sisters in the Lord are being persecuted and killed for their faith in Jesus. So many people die just because they happened to be born in the "wrong" place at the "wrong" time—during a famine, a war, or a time of civil upheaval. We ourselves may suffer exclusion or economic setbacks because of our faith. But Jesus wants to tell all of us that it will not last forever. We can hope in him and be patient a little bit longer.

"Heavenly Father, you hold this world in your hands. Your time and purposes are beyond our understanding. Nevertheless, I trust in you, my loving Father, to work all these things out for the good and for the salvation of the world. I trust in you, Father!"

Revelation 6:12-17

[12] When he opened the sixth seal, I looked, and there came a great earthquake; the sun became black as sackcloth, the full moon became like blood, [13]and the stars of the sky fell to the earth as the fig tree drops its winter fruit when shaken by a gale. [14]The sky vanished like a scroll rolling itself up, and every mountain and island was removed from its place. [15]Then the kings of the earth and the magnates and the generals and the rich and the powerful, and everyone, slave and free, hid in the caves and among the rocks of the mountains, [16]calling to the mountains and rocks, "Fall on us and hide us from the face of the one seated on the throne and from the wrath of the Lamb; [17]for the great day of their wrath has come, and who is able to stand?"

For the great day of their wrath has come, and who is able to stand?
(Revelation 6:17)

If we're honest, we would probably admit that when faced with the prospects of judgment, our first impulse is to hide. Just like the people in Revelation who called on the mountains to hide them, just like Adam and Eve who hid in the garden after they had sinned, we too can be afraid to submit ourselves to the all-seeing gaze of God.

When we read about the sixth seal—with its earthquakes, blackened sun, blood-red moon, falling stars, and other fearsome physical destruction—we may come to the conclusion that the judgment of God is a fearful and terrible thing. No wonder everyone on earth was made equal in his or her reaction to the coming punishment! How could we possibly hold our heads up when there are such powerful forces at work, forces that expose our weakness and sinfulness?

But in the midst of all this confusion and fearful imagery, don't forget that God didn't kill Adam and Eve; he *clothed* them and stayed with them, even in their exile from paradise. Similarly, before the widespread destruction in the Book of Revelation, God marked those who were his own (Revelation 7:1-8).

Where do you think you will turn in the face of God's powerful presence? You can try to run away from him, hoping that the mountains will cover you, or trying to find shelter in barren caves. Or you can run *toward* him for forgiveness, protection, and salvation. The judgment of God is nothing more than the manifestation of his truth—and the truth about God is that he is merciful as well as just. Running to Jesus is the best thing we could ever do, for he has redeemed us by his death and resurrection. Now risen in glory, he promises that all those who embrace him and his gospel need never be afraid.

Every day between now and the end of time is a day of judgment and revelation. Every day, God turns his gaze toward us and seeks to reveal his majesty and holiness to us. So we have to ask, "Where will I turn today?" Don't turn away from his gaze! Don't try to hide behind your work, your responsibilities. Don't seek shelter in the shaky security offered by the world and its philosophies. Instead, let God's presence uncover the sin that remains, so that when the final day comes you will be fully ready for his kingdom. Seek forgiveness and healing now, because what is coming is not destruction but full and complete redemption!

"Jesus, I don't want your second coming to be a source of fear for me. I give you the freedom to bring to light whatever sin might be constraining me, so that I can be free to hold my head high while I await the arrival of your glorious kingdom!"

Revelation 7:1-8

[1] After this I saw four angels standing at the four corners of the earth, holding back the four winds of the earth so that no wind could blow on earth or sea or against any tree. [2] I saw another angel ascending from the rising of the sun, having the seal of the living God, and he called with a loud voice to the four angels who had been given power to damage earth and sea, [3] saying, "Do not damage the earth or the sea or the trees, until we have marked the servants of our God with a seal on their foreheads."

[4] And I heard the number of those who were sealed, one hundred forty-four thousand, sealed out of every tribe of the people of Israel:

[5] From the tribe of Judah twelve thousand sealed,
from the tribe of Reuben twelve thousand,
from the tribe of Gad twelve thousand,
[6] from the tribe of Asher twelve thousand,
from the tribe of Naphtali twelve thousand,
from the tribe of Manasseh twelve thousand,
[7] from the tribe of Simeon twelve thousand,
from the tribe of Levi twelve thousand,
from the tribe of Issachar twelve thousand,
[8] from the tribe of Zebulun twelve thousand,
from the tribe of Joseph twelve thousand,
from the tribe of Benjamin twelve thousand sealed.

As he unfolds his rich tapestry of images in the Book of Revelation, John peppers his account with numbers. Modern readers can be tempted to look at them the same way we read census figures or other statistics. But as with other examples of apocalyptic literature, very large numbers tend to be symbolic of a great gathering of people before the throne of God. Such is partly the case in Revelation's reference to the 144,000 "sealed" as the "servants of our God" (Revelation 7:4, 3).

The effect is similar to the way today's movie directors filming a battle scene or natural disaster will "pan out" of the scene to reveal the full scope of the action. By pulling back in this way the director enables the audience to see the vast numbers involved in the struggle and appreciate the drama.

In another sense, however, while 144,000 represents a great multitude, there's another meaning beyond its sheer numeric value. It is a clue straight from salvation history. The figure, we're told, represents 12,000 from "every tribe of the people of Israel" (Revelation 7:4).

About seven hundred years before Revelation was written, nearly all the Israelite tribes were wiped out by the armies of Assyria. The few who survived the war went into exile, and many of those became assimilated into the surrounding countries and cultures. The last remnant was the kingdom of Judah, and it was subjected to war and exile another 140 years later. In John's day, just a small remnant remained around Jerusalem. Most of the other Jews lived throughout the Fertile Crescent. Then, in A.D. 70, Roman legions devastated Jerusalem itself, and the remaining Jewish refugees were scattered across the empire. Given this tragic history, what could be the meaning of 144,000 Israelites reappearing to serve God in the end of days?

This multitude of witnesses represents a promise fulfilled. God called Israel "my people." He made a covenant with Abraham and his children. He rescued them from slavery. He gave them the law and the prophets. John's vision recalls that of Ezekiel, who also foretold God would one day restore all the children of Israel, including those tribes lost to history. The 144,000 servants are a sign that God is faithful to his people.

From its inception, Revelation was a message of hope for those persecuted amid troubled times. The vision in this book unveils the truth that God has been in control of our destiny from the beginning, and that he is sure to achieve his purposes in the fullness of time. Knowing this, we can place our trust in the God who saves. Every prayer time is a new invitation to join in the worship at the heavenly throne. Meditating on God's faithfulness, we can rise above the setbacks we face, both personally and as a church.

"Lord, may my daily prayer give me the perspective of those marked with your seal. Help me to stand among your servants today, always ready to testify about your plan of salvation."

Revelation 7:9-17

9   After this I looked, and there was a great multitude that no one could count, from every nation, from all tribes and peoples and languages, standing before the throne and before the Lamb, robed in white, with palm branches in their hands. [10]They cried out in a loud voice, saying,

"Salvation belongs to our God who is seated on the throne,
    and to the Lamb!"
[11]And all the angels stood around the throne and around the elders and the four living creatures, and they fell on their faces before the throne and worshiped God, [12]singing,

"Amen! Blessing and glory and wisdom
and thanksgiving and honor
and power and might
be to our God forever and ever! Amen."
13   Then one of the elders addressed me, saying, "Who are these, robed in white, and where have they come from?" [14]I said to him, "Sir, you are the one that knows." Then he said to me, "These are they who have come out of the great ordeal; they have washed their robes and made them white in the blood of the Lamb.
15   For this reason they are before the throne of God,

and worship him day and night within his temple,
  and the one who is seated on the throne will shelter them.
16 They will hunger no more, and thirst no more;
  the sun will not strike them,
    nor any scorching heat;
17 for the Lamb at the center of the throne will be their shepherd,
    and he will guide them to springs of the water of life,
  and God will wipe away every tear from their eyes."

From the very beginning, the church has honored its martyrs and heroes. What began on a popular and local level gradually became woven into the liturgy, beginning around the fourth century in the eucharistic prayers. In the fifth century, a feast honoring all the saints was declared in some eastern churches, and from there the celebration was taken up in Rome. In A.D. 835, Pope Gregory IV declared All Saints Day a feast for the entire church.

A day commemorating the saints is actually a day of rejoicing in the greatness of the Lord and hoping in his love. The victory that we see in the saints testifies to the Lord himself. It was not just their own efforts that produced such holiness, but the work of the Lord, who wants to pour the fullness of the life of Jesus into our hearts. This has been the hope and joy of all holy men and women always and everywhere, and it is our hope and joy as well.

The Book of Revelation contains a vision of the redeemed of the Lord, gathered around the throne of God: "They have washed their robes and made them white in the blood of the Lamb" (Revelation 7:14). The victory of the redeemed came through the blood of Jesus, which washed them, purified them, and sealed them with the promise of eternal life.

The power of this precious blood of Christ is available to us every day by faith. We can turn to Jesus at any moment and ask for his blood to cover our sins and cleanse us. We can call on Jesus at any moment for him to pour out the power of his death and resurrection to strengthen us and enable us to live as God's children. "What love the Father has given us, that we should be called children of God" (1 John 3:1). We are his children; he has adopted us as his very own! Every day, our Father's hand is extended to us, and we have the great privilege to take hold of him.

Let us fix our eyes on the Lamb at the center of the throne, who has promised to be our shepherd and to lead us to "springs of the water of life" (Revelation 7:17). The Lord, who has worked in the lives of the saints, is ready to work in us if we will turn to him. Our God—who has chosen us to be his very own—is faithful!

Revelation 8:1-5

¹ When the Lamb opened the seventh seal, there was silence in heaven for about half an hour. ²And I saw the seven angels who stand before God, and seven trumpets were given to them.
³ Another angel with a golden censer came and stood at the altar; he was given a great quantity of incense to offer with the prayers of all the saints on the golden altar that is before the throne. ⁴And the smoke of the incense, with the prayers of the saints, rose before God from the hand of the angel. ⁵Then the angel took the censer and filled it with fire from the altar and threw it on the earth; and there were peals of thunder, rumblings, flashes of lightning, and an earthquake.

The opening of the seventh seal comes at the end of a long, turbulent cycle of events. It follows John's description of the terrible four horses and their path of destruction and pestilence, as well as earthquakes and other natural disasters. It also follows the momentous gathering of the 144,000 witnesses and the great multitude.

Such a buildup makes what happens next seem all the more striking: "When the Lamb opened the seventh seal, there was silence in heaven" (Revelation 8:1). Silence! Not a grand entrance or great calamity. Just a thoughtful, sober quietness in heaven.

This dramatic silence recalls an earlier epiphany of God described in the Old Testament. When God commanded Elijah to await his presence on the mountaintop, the prophet first beheld a shattering windstorm, followed by earthquakes, and then a great fire—but the Lord did not appear in any of those. It was only when Elijah heard the sound of a low whisper, Scripture says, that he hid his face in his cloak. Elijah knew for certain that in that small stillness, he was in the presence of the Holy One of Israel (see 1 Kings 19:11-13).

The echo of that small stillness here, in John's vision of the end times, is another example of how his testimony is deeply rooted in Scripture. His sweeping grasp of the word of God is the foundation and source of his interpretation of what lies ahead in salvation history—and it is also the foundation for his sense of hope and trust. After all, God never abandoned Israel. Why would he abandon his church?

Following this interlude of silence, a new cycle opens, that of the seven angels bearing seven trumpets (Revelation 8:2). Once again, John described prayer as the catalyst for this new cycle. He wrote that he saw an angel who "stood at the altar" with a golden censer filled with incense, "and the smoke of the incense, with the prayers of the saints, rose before God from the hand of the angel" (8:4).

This brief interlude of quietness and prayer in heaven is an invitation to reflect on our own attitude toward prayer. There are times when we need to quiet our souls before God, and to listen for his word. John's vision of heaven recalls the words of the psalm, "Be still, and know that I am God!" (Psalm 46:10). John's vision invites us, the people of faith, not to fear or be anxious but to rest in God and place all our trust in him.

"Lord Jesus, like the multitude of heaven before your throne, I want to quiet my soul before you. Teach me to put aside all cares and concerns as I come into your presence. As I learn to be still before you, let your love fill me with the certainty of your saving power."

Seven Trumpets, One Scroll, and Two Prophets

Revelation 8:6–11:19

Seven Trumpets, One Scroll, and Two Prophets
Revelation 8:6–11:19

Revelation 8:6-13

6 Now the seven angels who had the seven trumpets made ready to blow them.

7 The first angel blew his trumpet, and there came hail and fire, mixed with blood, and they were hurled to the earth; and a third of the earth was burned up, and a third of the trees were burned up, and all green grass was burned up.

8 The second angel blew his trumpet, and something like a great mountain, burning with fire, was thrown into the sea. 9A third of the sea became blood, a third of the living creatures in the sea died, and a third of the ships were destroyed.

10 The third angel blew his trumpet, and a great star fell from heaven, blazing like a torch, and it fell on a third of the rivers and on the springs of water. 11The name of the star is Wormwood. A third of the waters became wormwood, and many died from the water, because it was made bitter.

12 The fourth angel blew his trumpet, and a third of the sun was struck, and a third of the moon, and a third of the stars, so that a third of their light was darkened; a third of the day was kept from shining, and likewise the night.

13 Then I looked, and I heard an eagle crying with a loud voice as it flew in midheaven, "Woe, woe, woe to the inhabitants of the earth, at the blasts of the other trumpets that the three angels are about to blow!"

Similar to other apocalyptic writing in Scripture, Revelation is teeming with allusions to Old Testament passages. It almost seems as if John's vision is reverberating with echoes straight out of the history of God's people. These verses are a good example of this resonance with Israel's past. The angels sounding their trumpets are reminiscent of those trumpets used by Joshua's army to destroy Jericho (see Joshua 6). Just as Joshua's trumpets signaled the end of the ancient and well-fortified city of Jericho, the angelic trumpets of Revelation herald that the old order of things is giving way to a new creation.

John wrote that at the first trumpet blast, "hail and fire, mixed with blood" were thrown upon the earth. "A third of the earth was burned up," as well (Revelation 8:7). Each subsequent blast unleashed another calamity: He saw a mountain of fire appear, a third of the sea turn to blood, and a third of the light from the sun, moon, and stars go out (8:8-13). These disasters evoke the plagues of the book of Exodus, when God turned the Nile into blood and brought other afflictions on the Egyptians because of Pharaoh's stubbornness. But just as Pharaoh hardened his heart to God in spite of these signs from heaven, John understood that even in the end times there will continue to be many who refuse to heed God's calls to repentance.

John's use of recurring images from Scripture is a clear signal that the future will not be some arbitrary re-design or change of course on God's part. Instead, the end of history should be seen as the fruition of God's handiwork throughout all time. In other words, by faith we are to perceive that the future constitutes a sort of "final episode" of salvation history, not an abrupt departure from God's plan. John's vision is part of a cohesive fabric: one, single, unified panorama of God's saving action from beginning to end.

One of the challenging aspects of reading the Book of Revelation is this: Can we root ourselves in the word of God just as John did? Can we grasp firmly onto this panorama of salvation history and allow our very outlook on the future to be shaped by God's promises in the past and his faithfulness in the present? We can confidently say yes, because the Holy Spirit can bring the Scriptures alive in our hearts. So turn to the Spirit today and ask him to anchor your life—past, present, and future—in Christ.

"Come, Holy Spirit! Let the word of God burn in my heart. Let it purify my mind and teach me deeply that I am made to live with you forever."

Revelation 9:1-12

¹ And the fifth angel blew his trumpet, and I saw a star that had fallen from heaven to earth, and he was given the key to the shaft of the bottomless pit; ²he opened the shaft of the bottomless pit, and from the shaft rose smoke like the smoke of a great furnace, and the sun and the air were darkened with the smoke from the shaft. ³Then from the smoke came locusts on the earth, and they were given authority like the authority of scorpions of the earth. ⁴They were told not to damage the grass of the earth or any green growth or any tree, but only those people who do not have the seal of God on their foreheads. ⁵They were allowed to torture them for five months, but not to kill them, and their torture was like the torture of a scorpion when it stings someone. ⁶And in those days people will seek death but will not find it; they will long to die, but death will flee from them.
⁷ In appearance the locusts were like horses equipped for battle. On their heads were what looked like crowns of gold; their faces were like human faces, ⁸their hair like women's hair, and their teeth like lions' teeth; ⁹they had scales like iron breastplates, and the noise of their wings was like the noise of many chariots with horses rushing into battle. ¹⁰They have tails like scorpions, with stingers, and in their tails is their power to harm people for five months. ¹¹They

have as king over them the angel of the bottomless pit; his name in Hebrew is Abaddon, and in Greek he is called Apollyon.

¹² The first woe has passed. There are still two woes to come.

War! Violence! Destruction! Images of conflict assault our senses when we read many parts of Revelation—like this account of the plague of bizarre locusts sent by the "angel of the bottomless pit" (Revelation 9:11).

What is the purpose of reflecting on such troubling passages? One reason is that their disturbing and turbulent imagery are grounded in a spiritual reality that we all face. As Christians, we have to acknowledge that we are in a very real battle against sin and evil. The call to discipleship entails struggling against temptation and our rebellious nature—what Saint Paul called "the flesh"—as well as standing up to unrighteous behavior.

If we're honest, we will admit that it is often easier to dismiss this spiritual struggle. As long as we can maintain an outward calm and peacefulness, can't we let a few things slide? That's exactly the attitude that these visions from Revelation challenge. John's message about the deadly consequences of sin compels us to ask, Am I really in this fight? Am I willing to take a few lumps if it means holding fast to Jesus and preparing myself for his kingdom?

It might help to consider an example from the lives of the saints. Ignatius of Loyola was once a soldier who fought in earthly battles. In his landmark treatise, the *Spiritual Exercises*, Ignatius took his cue from those battles to describe the spiritual battle that every Christian faces. In one meditation, he described the world as being divided between two standards. One standard is held aloft by Lucifer and the other by Christ. Each side actively sends out forces to patrol the world. One goes armed with "nets and chains" to ensnare souls, the other uses the word of God to free humanity from the snares of the devil. If we choose Christ's standard, Ignatius said, then we accept him as our "Commander in Chief" and must become wholehearted combatants on this battlefield.

Ignatius also wrote that, as with those who serve earthly kings, Jesus enlists his followers to fight for his cause:

> How much more worthy of consideration is it to see Christ our Lord, the Eternal King, and before him, all mankind, to whom and to each man in particular, he calls, and says: "It is my will to conquer the whole world and all my enemies, and thus to enter into the glory of my Father. Whoever would like to come with me must labor with me, so that following me in suffering, he may also follow me in glory." (*Spiritual Exercises*, Second Week, Exercise 95)

Today, remember that you are called to lift high the banner of Christ in your struggle against sin. Remember, too, that victory can be yours as you cling to Christ, your captain and standard-bearer.

"Lord Jesus, I know you are at my side in spiritual combat. I ask you to keep me strong in resisting sin."

Revelation 9:13-21

13 Then the sixth angel blew his trumpet, and I heard a voice from the four horns of the golden altar before God, 14saying to the sixth angel who had the trumpet, "Release the four angels who are bound at the great river Euphrates." 15So the four angels were released, who had been held ready for the hour, the day, the month, and the year, to kill a third of humankind. 16The number of the troops of cavalry was two hundred million; I heard their number. 17And this was how I saw the horses in my vision: the riders wore breastplates the color of fire and of sapphire and of sulfur; the heads of the horses were like

lions' heads, and fire and smoke and sulfur came out of their mouths. [18]By these three plagues a third of humankind was killed, by the fire and smoke and sulfur coming out of their mouths. [19]For the power of the horses is in their mouths and in their tails; their tails are like serpents, having heads; and with them they inflict harm. [20] The rest of humankind, who were not killed by these plagues, did not repent of the works of their hands or give up worshiping demons and idols of gold and silver and bronze and stone and wood, which cannot see or hear or walk. [21]And they did not repent of their murders or their sorceries or their fornication or their thefts.

Besides its vivid descriptions of natural disasters and plagues, John's vision in Revelation is a heartbreaking commentary on the hardheartedness of humanity. In this passage, for example, John reports that, even after numerous afflictions fell upon the earth, the "rest of humankind, who were not killed by these plagues, did not repent of the works of their hands" (Revelation 9:20).

This sobering reflection was echoed in our own times by Pope John Paul II. In an apostolic exhortation entitled *Reconciliatio et Paenitentia* (Reconciliation and Penance), he described a looming spiritual crisis and warned that we must fight against a modern "eclipse of the conscience." He wrote,

> Too many signs indicate that such an eclipse exists in our time.
> . . . In this situation there is an obscuring also of the sense of
> sin, which is closely connected with the moral conscience, the
> search for truth and the desire to make a responsible use of
> freedom. When the conscience is weakened the sense of God
> is also obscured, and as a result, with the loss of this decisive
> inner point of reference, the sense of sin is lost. This explains
> why my predecessor Pius XI, one day declared, in words that

have almost become proverbial, that "the sin of the century is the loss of the sense of sin." (18)

The pope's exhortation went on to cite how this loss of the sense of sin can be tied to the rise of secularism, the acceptance of a new relativism in regard to morality, and a general abandonment of personal responsibility. But, John Paul wrote, this "mystery of sin" is countered in every age by the church, which proclaims Christ himself, the *mysterium pietatis*, the "mystery of our religion" (see 1 Timothy 3:16). John Paul continued:

Man's sin would be the winner and in the end destructive, [and] God's salvific plan would remain incomplete or even totally defeated, if this *mysterium pietatis* were not made part of the dynamism of history in order to conquer man's sin. (19)

We know that we, the church, must proclaim this saving mystery. As the vision of Revelation touches our hearts, it can move us to pray for the world. We can plead with the Spirit to enlighten the hearts and consciences of all people to turn back to God.

So, today, go before the Lord as a prayer warrior claiming the cleansing power of the blood of Christ over humanity. Be bold enough to ask God to send you out as witnesses to save the lost and bring them home to the Father.

"Lord, I proclaim your victory over all forms of sin and evil. May your Holy Spirit move my heart to witness to your plan of salvation."

Revelation 10:1-7

¹ And I saw another mighty angel coming down from heaven, wrapped in a cloud, with a rainbow over his head; his face was like the sun, and his legs like pillars of fire. ²He held a little scroll open in his hand. Setting his right foot on the sea and his left foot on the land, ³he gave a great shout, like a lion roaring. And when he shouted, the seven thunders sounded. ⁴And when the seven thunders had sounded, I was about to write, but I heard a voice from heaven saying, "Seal up what the seven thunders have said, and do not write it down." ⁵Then the angel whom I saw standing on the sea and the land

raised his right hand to heaven
⁶   and swore by him who lives
            forever and ever,

who created heaven and what is in it, the earth and what is in it, and the sea and what is in it: "There will be no more delay, ⁷but in the days when the seventh angel is to blow his trumpet, the mystery of God will be fulfilled, as he announced to his servants the prophets."

In chapter ten of Revelation, we encounter yet another cycle of symbolic signs. It begins with the coming of "another mighty angel" bearing a "little scroll" (Revelation 10:1-2), which John eventually will be asked to eat as part of his commission. This angel swears with a voice like thunder, "There will be no more delay," but that the "mystery of God will be fulfilled, as he announced to his servants the prophets" (10:6-7).

Scripture scholars are unclear if this section is part of the cycle of trumpets or if it is an interlude, like others that appear elsewhere in the book. But as hard as it may be to comprehend the dizzying array of symbols in John's apocalyptic language, the message of the angel is clear: God will fulfill his words! The world will end, and Christ will come again! May there be no more delay!

Embracing that prophetic stance is essential for each one of us. In a sermon reflecting on the end times, Fr. Raniero Cantalamessa, the preacher to the papal household, observed, "It would be the greatest foolishness to console oneself by saying that no one knows when the end of the world will be and forgetting that . . . it could be this very night."

In discussing Jesus' words to his disciples about the second coming, Fr. Cantalamessa said,

> In the gospel, Jesus assures us of the fact of his return and the gathering of his chosen ones from the "four winds"; the when and the how of his return (on the clouds between the darkening of the sun and the falling of the stars) is part of the figurative language of the literary genre of these discourses. . . .
>
> We must, I think, completely change the attitude with which we listen to these . . . [readings] that speak of the end of the world and the return of Christ. . . . The recurrent talk about the end of the world, which is often engaged in by those with a distorted religious sentiment, has a devastating effect on many people. It reinforces the idea of a God who is always angry, ready to vent his wrath on the world. But this is not the God of the Bible, which a psalm describes as "merciful and gracious, slow to anger and abounding in steadfast love, who will not always accuse or keep his anger forever . . . because he knows that we are made of dust" (Psalm 103:8-14). ("On the End of the World," 33rd Sunday in Ordinary Time, B)

"Father, your Spirit in my heart echoes the words of the angel: There should be no more delay! Come, Lord Jesus, and establish your reign of love over my heart and over all of humanity."

Revelation 10:8-11

⁸ Then the voice that I had heard from heaven spoke to me again, saying, "Go, take the scroll that is open in the hand of the angel who is standing on the sea and on the land." ⁹So I went to the angel and told him to give me the little scroll; and he said to me, "Take it, and eat; it will be bitter to your stomach, but sweet as honey in your mouth." ¹⁰So I took the little scroll from the hand of the angel and ate it; it was sweet as honey in my mouth, but when I had eaten it, my stomach was made bitter.
¹¹ Then they said to me, "You must prophesy again about many peoples and nations and languages and kings."

We can better understand why John was commanded to eat the scroll of God's word if we think of the words he was to proclaim to God's people (Revelation 10:9). As one who was to announce God's message, John had first to absorb the words on the scroll into his heart and mind. Then he had to allow it to nourish his spiritual life before he could effectively proclaim it.

Christians must be fed by God's word if they are to live it and proclaim it to others. Recognizing that, the Fathers of the Second Vatican Council exhorted all believers to "learn by frequent reading of the divine Scriptures the 'excellent knowledge of Jesus Christ.'" The council fathers believed that Christians "should gladly put themselves in touch with the sacred text." And they urged believers to heed the warning of the great Scripture scholar St. Jerome: "Ignorance of the Scriptures is ignorance of Christ" (*Dei Verbum*, 25).

Such seriousness is required when we recall what Scripture is: God's eternal word given to his people. Scripture reveals the mysteries of the Trinity—the divine characteristics of Father, Son, and Holy Spirit. God's character shines forth from Scripture—his sovereignty, glory, might, and love. Scripture unfolds God's wondrous plan for creation; our fullness and centeredness in the Son, our redemption and restoration to the divine image through the work of the cross; the enlivening we receive through the indwelling of the Spirit. Scripture provides the nourishment our spirits crave. With this food, we experience a richer life in God.

Admittedly, reading Scripture may sometimes challenge us. The angel told John that the scroll would be "bitter to your stomach, but sweet as honey in your mouth" (Revelation 10:9). Scripture can seem "bitter" to us because it challenges us to change our lives and live in conformity with the will of God. Yet, at the same time, it is sweet because it helps us to know God and his tender love. As we take up the scroll of life and "eat" of it, let us trust God's promise that his word will taste like honey in our mouths even if it may prove bitter to our stomachs as we accept the challenges it puts before us. We can take comfort in the promise that the "bitterness" lasts but a short while; the sweetness is eternal and unfading.

Revelation 11:1-14

¹ Then I was given a measuring rod like a staff, and I was told, "Come and measure the temple of God and the altar and those who worship there, ²but do not measure the court outside the temple; leave that out, for it is given over to the nations, and they will trample over the holy city for forty-two months. ³And I will grant my two witnesses authority to prophesy for one thousand two hundred sixty days, wearing sackcloth."

⁴ These are the two olive trees and the two lampstands that stand before the Lord of the earth. ⁵And if anyone wants to harm them, fire pours from their mouth and consumes their foes; anyone who wants to harm them must be killed in this manner. ⁶They have

authority to shut the sky, so that no rain may fall during the days of their prophesying, and they have authority over the waters to turn them into blood, and to strike the earth with every kind of plague, as often as they desire.

7   When they have finished their testimony, the beast that comes up from the bottomless pit will make war on them and conquer them and kill them, 8and their dead bodies will lie in the street of the great city that is prophetically called Sodom and Egypt, where also their Lord was crucified. 9For three and a half days members of the peoples and tribes and languages and nations will gaze at their dead bodies and refuse to let them be placed in a tomb; 10and the inhabitants of the earth will gloat over them and celebrate and exchange presents, because these two prophets had been a torment to the inhabitants of the earth.

11   But after the three and a half days, the breath of life from God entered them, and they stood on their feet, and those who saw them were terrified. 12Then they heard a loud voice from heaven saying to them, "Come up here!" And they went up to heaven in a cloud while their enemies watched them. 13At that moment there was a great earthquake, and a tenth of the city fell; seven thousand people were killed in the earthquake, and the rest were terrified and gave glory to the God of heaven.

14   The second woe has passed. The third woe is coming very soon.

The legal codes of antiquity required at least two witnesses to give testimony. In his description of "what must take place" (Revelation 4:1), John described God raising up two such witnesses with the "authority to prophesy" (11:3) against the corruption in the world. The two are never directly identified, but we know them by their works: like Moses, they have the power to "smite the earth with every plague," and like Elijah, they will be able to "shut the sky" (11:6). In the power of these two greatest prophets, the witnesses serve to strengthen those who have remained faithful to the Lord.

The structure of this passage follows a typical pattern in Jewish literature: the wicked besiege God's witnesses, but God exalts his own and defeats the unrighteous. After completing their allotted time of testimony, the witnesses are killed by the beast from the bottomless pit. Faithfully did they serve; obediently did they testify. Now, the Lord has called them to his side, while he executes his judgment against those on earth who opposed these two men.

The witnesses' corpses are left unburied—polluting a city that has developed into "Sodom and Egypt" (Revelation 11:8). The unrighteous may revel in their seeming victory, but their celebration is short-lived. After three and a half days, "the breath of life from God" resurrects the witnesses and brings them safe to heaven. Out of great fear, the unrighteous glorify Yahweh, but it is too late for them.

John's vision reveals that there will be times when the people of God will suffer setbacks, apparent defeats, and even tragedy. But God's servants can never be defeated! Moses and Elijah proved this in their lifetimes, and it seems that they will do so once again during the birth pangs of the new Jerusalem. When we are beset by failure or confused about the path we should take, when we feel discouraged or even defeated, we should recall this vision. The beast's victory was not the final word. Hold on to your faith and do not lose hope under stressful circumstances. The Lord of history will vindicate his righteous ones.

"Lord, we count it a privilege to follow you in good times and bad. We surrender ourselves to you with the prayer of your Son, Jesus: 'Not my will, Father, but your will be done.'"

Revelation 11:15-19

[15] Then the seventh angel blew his trumpet, and there were loud voices in heaven, saying,

"The kingdom of the world has
　　become the kingdom of our Lord
　and of his Messiah,
and he will reign forever and ever."

[16] Then the twenty-four elders who sit on their thrones before God fell on their faces and worshiped God, [17]singing,

"We give you thanks, Lord God Almighty,
　who are and who were,
for you have taken your great power
　and begun to reign.

[18] The nations raged,
　　but your wrath has come,
　　and the time for judging the dead,
　for rewarding your servants,
　　　the prophets
　and saints and all who fear your name,
　　both small and great,
　and for destroying those who
　　　destroy the earth."

[19] Then God's temple in heaven was opened, and the ark of his covenant was seen within his temple; and there were flashes of lightning, rumblings, peals of thunder, an earthquake, and heavy hail.

"The kingdom of the world has become the kingdom of our Lord
and of his Messiah, and he will reign forever and ever."
(Revelation 11:15)

What a marvelous declaration! John described hearing this great affirmation following the seventh trumpet blast. In response, the twenty-four elders "fell on their faces and worshiped God" (Revelation 11:16) and voiced all of heaven's thanks to the Lord Almighty for judging the world, rewarding his "servants, the prophets and saints . . . and for destroying those who destroy the earth" (11:18).

This extended interlude of praise marks a welcome respite after the battles, plagues, earthquakes, and other tragic events heralded by the previous six trumpets. Actually, Revelation is filled with similar passages, such as the spontaneous bursts of adoration by the elders and the heavenly host (see Revelation 4:11; 5:9; and 6:10, for example). Longer passages of exaltation and veneration also appear throughout John's narrative, forming a regular counterpoint to the many tribulations he describes (see 7:12; 12:10; 14:6; 15:3).

In fact, such episodes of worship are a natural and fitting part of John's vision of what lies ahead for humanity. John understood that from the beginning the human race was formed to praise God. He saw that those who had been baptized and sealed with the mark of faith would someday take their rightful place with the heavenly host worshiping God.

St. Augustine of Hippo echoed this vision when he wrote, "Great are you, O Lord, and greatly to be praised. . . . And man, being a part of your creation, desires to praise you. . . . You move us to delight in praising you" (*Confessions*, Chapter 1).

Every day, God invites us to spend time with him, and not just so that we can bring him our petitions and intercessions. He wants us to make praise and quiet listening a consistent part of our prayer lives. And our greatest opportunity is our communal worship in the

liturgy of the Mass. This is, after all, a foretaste of the wedding supper of the Lamb that awaits us!

What's more, also in accord with John's message, we should get
in the habit of praising God during those times when we struggle to
overcome sin and unrighteousness. Like the author of Revelation,
St. Augustine also lived in a time of chaos, when the Roman empire
was starting to collapse all around him. These saints are both witnesses to us that we can praise and exalt God no matter what our
circumstances.

"Lord, you formed us for yourself, and we praise you. Our hearts long
to enter your courts in worship and thanksgiving. All honor, blessing,
praise, and glory be unto you, Father, Son, and Holy Spirit!"

The Woman, the Beasts, and the Harvest

Revelation 12:1–15:4

The Woman, the Beasts, and the Harvest
Revelation 12:1–15:4

Revelation 12:1-6

¹ A great portent appeared in heaven: a woman clothed with the sun, with the moon under her feet, and on her head a crown of twelve stars. ²She was pregnant and was crying out in birthpangs, in the agony of giving birth. ³Then another portent appeared in heaven: a great red dragon, with seven heads and ten horns, and seven diadems on his heads. ⁴His tail swept down a third of the stars of heaven and threw them to the earth. Then the dragon stood before the woman who was about to bear a child, so that he might devour her child as soon as it was born. ⁵And she gave birth to a son, a male child, who is to rule all the nations with a rod of iron. But her child was snatched away and taken to God and to his throne; ⁶and the woman fled into the wilderness, where she has a place prepared by God, so that there she can be nourished for one thousand two hundred sixty days.

With the conclusion of the seventh trumpet blast, John's narrative has reached a turning point. God's judgment has been announced, warnings from heaven have been given, and now the kingdom of the world is about to become the kingdom of our Lord. The stage is now set for the climactic battle that will bring about the victory of good over evil. Let's backtrack just a bit so that we can get a better perspective on this pivotal moment.

The symbolic signs of this imminent battle form a "cycle-within-a-cycle" in the midst of the angelic trumpets. First, a mighty angel appeared bearing a "small scroll," which John ate, signifying his divine commission to testify to the conclusive events about to unfold (see Revelation 10:1-11).

Next, John described measuring God's temple, the two witnesses sent by God, and the heavenly declaration about the new kingdom that is on the horizon (see Revelation 11:1-15). Finally, John saw the ark of the covenant revealed as God's temple was opened (see 11:19).

Seen sequentially, these events signal the approach of the final battle that will end the course of human history as we know it and bring about the final age.

But wait. On the cusp of battle, John saw in heaven a terrible, personal confrontation. A "woman clothed with the sun" (Revelation 12:1), who was about to deliver a child, is besieged by "a great red dragon" laying in wait to devour her child (12:3-4).

This one image depicts humankind's agelong struggle. For the dragon is identified a few lines later as none other than "Satan" (Revelation 12:9), and his assault on the woman signifies his long enmity against the people of God. What's more, just as the woman's plight illustrates our condition, so does her deliverance. Her "male child" is caught up to God's throne, and she herself escapes to safety in a place prepared for her by God (see 12:5-6).

Now, having given a name and a face to the foe behind all the sinful conduct leading up to this point, John's story plows ahead to describe the great war between Satan and his two henchmen against the Lamb and his army of 144,000 witness and the angelic host led by the archangel Michael.

The imagery is insistent: to understand our destiny, we need look to our origins. God made us to be with him from the beginning. And even though we are now engaged in a struggle with sin and unrighteousness, God will not fail us in the end. The Lord remains our deliverer, yesterday, today, and forever!

"Lord, strengthen me so that I can reach out to those who are still in anguish because they do not know your plan of salvation."

Revelation 12:7-12

[7] And war broke out in heaven; Michael and his angels fought against the dragon. The dragon and his angels fought back, [8]but they were defeated, and there was no longer any place for them in heaven. [9]The great dragon was thrown down, that ancient serpent, who is called the Devil and Satan, the deceiver of the whole world—he was thrown down to the earth, and his angels were thrown down with him.

[10] Then I heard a loud voice in heaven, proclaiming,

"Now have come the salvation and the power
    and the kingdom of our God
    and the authority of his Messiah,
for the accuser of our comrades has been thrown down,
    who accuses them day and night before our God.
[11] But they have conquered him by the blood of the Lamb
    and by the word of their testimony,
for they did not cling to life even in the face of death.
[12] Rejoice then, you heavens
    and those who dwell in them!
But woe to the earth and the sea,
    for the devil has come down to you
with great wrath,
    because he knows that his time is short!"

Bless the Lord, all you his angels, his ministers who do his will.
(Gospel Acclamation)

In the beginning, God created earth and stars, sun and moon, plants and animals, humans and angels. It is easy to forget these last, since they belong to a mysterious world that we neither see nor perceive. Yet, as surely as God created the physical realm in which we live, he also created a spiritual domain in which angels sing his praises and act according to his will (see Revelation 12:7, 10-11).

It is important to recall that there is a world beyond what we can see. Life—eternal life—extends beyond the physical world. That spiritual world is central to our Christian belief. In some way, archangels and angels are engaged in spiritual warfare in their service to God (see Revelation 12:7-12; Jude 9). They minister to God as he gathers his people to himself (see 1 Thessalonians 4:16). God is far grater than anything we can imagine. So, too, is his creation! All too easily, we narrow our thinking and existence to what we can apprehend objectively. Let us rather turn our minds to God and allow him to expand our understanding.

Archangels are servants of God, dedicated to carrying out his word with their whole being. They are his emissaries, his messengers sent on our behalf. Each of the archangels has been entrusted with important service. To Michael, the archangel, are given acts of power through which he provides refuge, preserves us from fear, and bestows peace (Revelation 12:7-10). Gabriel, "the strength of God," reveals God's word, as to Zechariah and the Virgin Mary (see Luke 1:11-20, 26-38). Raphael was sent from God as the "medicine of God," healing sinful hearts and guiding them to God (Tobit 12:6-22).

The archangels serve, guard, and guide. They are faithful, farsighted, and powerful, and God has given them a crucial role to play. The archangels and angels are part of God's wonderful plan of life. Submitted to God and his plan, they serve to advance his work in ways we can only glimpse. Let us be thankful for the work they do in fulfilling God's plan to restore us as his sons and daughters. Let us rejoice with the church, "Bless the Lord, all you his angels, his ministers who do his will."

Revelation 12:13-18

¹³ So when the dragon saw that he had been thrown down to the earth, he pursued the woman who had given birth to the male child. ¹⁴But the woman was given the two wings of the great eagle, so that she could fly from the serpent into the wilderness, to her place where she is nourished for a time, and times, and half a time. ¹⁵Then from his mouth the serpent poured water like a river after the woman, to sweep her away with the flood. ¹⁶But the earth came to the help of the woman; it opened its mouth and swallowed the river that the dragon had poured from his mouth. ¹⁷Then the dragon was angry with the woman, and went off to make war on the rest of her children, those who keep the commandments of God and hold the testimony of Jesus.
¹⁸ Then the dragon took his stand on the sand of the seashore.

Today we should echo heaven's triumphal shout: "Now have come the salvation and the power and the kingdom of our God and the authority of his Messiah" (Revelation 12:10). This victory is not something long, long ago, nor is it far off in the future. It is ours—now! Rejoice and praise God, and ask the Holy Spirit to make these words come alive in you heart every day.

John left no doubt about how the saints achieved victory over Satan: "They have conquered him by the blood of the Lamb" (Revelation 12:11). The sacrifice of Jesus' body and blood on the cross is our salvation. We must bear testimony to his saving power by living righteously.

John was not closing his eyes to the daily struggle against sin when he painted such a triumphant picture. He reaffirmed that believers on the earth must vigilantly guard themselves against the evil one, who is furious "because he knows that his time is short!" (Revelation 12:12). He described Satan's pursuit of "the woman who had given birth to the male child" (12:13) and his longstanding war against her offspring, "those who keep the commandments of God and hold the testimony of Jesus" (12:17).

It bears mentioning that this mysterious woman of Revelation 12 has long been a source of speculation. Some say she represents the church. Others believe she stands for all of humanity. There is also a Catholic tradition that associates her in some way with Mary, the mother of God. Often such connections draw parallels between Mary and Eve from the book of Genesis. Both women contended with "that ancient serpent" (Revelation 12:9). But whereas Eve disobeyed God and gave birth to a fallen race, Mary obeyed the Lord and brought forth Jesus, King of the new creation.

The saints triumphed "by the blood of the Lamb"; similarly, St. Lawrence of Brindisi, a sixteenth century doctor of the church, wrote that Mary was "clothed with the sun" by the work of Jesus: "It was from the child in her womb that Mary received all her glory. He clothed her with the sun, rolled the moon beneath her feet, and set upon her head a crown" (from the *Mariale*, Sermon 6).

So many different interpretations of this passage from Revelation are possible precisely because apocalyptic writing uses so many layers of symbolism. The vivid, figurative language of Revelation was intended to help the early Christians look beyond their trials and sufferings and see the victory that Jesus, the Lamb of God, had already won for all of us. By contemplating these mysteries today, we too can have our hearts lifted up.

"Lamb of God, Holy One, we proclaim that your blood has washed away our sins. May you take your rightful place on the throne of our hearts, today and forever."

Revelation 13:1-10

¹ And I saw a beast rising out of the sea having ten horns and seven heads; and on its horns were ten diadems, and on its heads were blasphemous names. ²And the beast that I saw was like a leopard, its feet were like a bear's, and its mouth was like a lion's mouth. And the dragon gave it his power and his throne and great authority. ³One of its heads seemed to have received a death-blow, but its mortal wound had been healed. In amazement the whole earth followed the beast. ⁴They worshiped the dragon, for he had given his authority to the beast, and they worshiped the beast, saying, "Who is like the beast, and who can fight against it?"

⁵ The beast was given a mouth uttering haughty and blasphemous words, and it was allowed to exercise authority for forty-two months. ⁶It opened its mouth to utter blasphemies against God, blaspheming his name and his dwelling, that is, those who dwell in heaven. ⁷Also it was allowed to make war on the saints and to conquer them. It was given authority over every tribe and people and language and nation, ⁸and all the inhabitants of the earth will worship it, everyone whose name has not been written from the foundation of the world in the book of life of the Lamb that was slaughtered.

⁹ Let anyone who has an ear listen:

¹⁰ If you are to be taken captive,
  into captivity you go;
 if you kill with the sword,
  with the sword you must be killed.
Here is a call for the endurance and faith of the saints.

If you want to find a key to understanding this graphic description of the beast, you need to persevere to the last sentence of this passage: "Here is a call for the endurance and faith of the saints."

This description of a beast rising out of the sea—identified throughout the Old Testament as the place of chaos, evil, and opposition to God—contains several allusions to the anti-Christian world power of the author's day, the Roman Empire. A legend even said that the emperor Nero didn't really commit suicide but had fled to the east and would return to power. We can substitute whatever "evil empire" most terrifies us in the twenty-first century if we want to appreciate the lesson of endurance and faith that undergirds this passage.

This beast, given authority by the dragon (Satan), is indeed awe-inspiring. It combines features of earth's most vicious animals, its mouth spews forth blasphemy, and it has miraculously recovered from a mortal wound. No wonder everyone on earth (perhaps a little peer pressure here?) worships it. Everyone, that is, whose name isn't written in the Lamb's book of life. Faced with such a reality, terror and anxiety seem perfectly reasonable human responses.

And yet the terrible authority of the beast is limited by the omnipotent Lord to a short time, the proverbial forty-two months. Clearly, evil will not reign forever, and those who remain faithful to the light of Christ will see the darkness dissipate.

If we are to survive direct persecution and remain loyal to God in a hostile environment, we need to have faith in the slain Lamb, who has overcome death itself along with all the lesser "deaths" that tempt us to despair. We need to be able to look beyond our current challenges and see God working out our salvation in the midst of dark circumstances.

Where is my gaze fixed today? Is it fixed on the present difficulties that can make me feel isolated, or on Jesus' presence in and with me always (see Matthew 28:20)? On my trials, or on the triumph Jesus promised (see John 16:33)? On my weaknesses, or on the faithfulness of God who provides a way of escape in every temptation (see 1 Corinthians 10:13)?

Also, where am I dwelling? Do I dwell "on earth" (Revelation 13:8), where I submit to false values like everyone else? Or do I understand that my true home even now is with "those who dwell in heaven," where God is already reigning (13:6) until the entire world acknowledges his authority?

"Who is like you, Lord, majestic in holiness, terrible in glorious deeds, doing wonders? In your steadfast love you have led the people you have redeemed. You have guided us by your strength to your holy dwelling. Help me enjoy the security of dwelling in your presence and praising you continuously."

Revelation 13:11-18

[11] Then I saw another beast that rose out of the earth; it had two horns like a lamb and it spoke like a dragon. [12]It exercises all the authority of the first beast on its behalf, and it makes the earth and its inhabitants worship the first beast, whose mortal wound had been healed. [13]It performs great signs, even making fire come down from heaven to earth in the sight of all; [14]and by the signs that it is allowed to perform on behalf of the beast, it deceives the inhabitants of earth, telling them to make an image for the beast that had been wounded by the sword and yet lived; [15]and it was allowed to give breath to the image of the beast so that the image of the beast could even speak and cause those who would not worship the image of the beast to be killed. [16]Also it causes all, both small and great, both rich and poor, both free and slave, to be marked on the right hand or the forehead, [17]so that no one can buy or sell who does not have the mark, that is, the name of the beast or the number of its name. [18]This calls for wisdom: let anyone with understanding calculate the number of the beast, for it is the number of a person. Its number is six hundred sixty-six.

Whose mark do you bear, the generic mark of the beast or the personal name of the Lamb?

Although various interpretations of the number 666 have been proposed, the most likely is that it stood for Caesar Nero; if each letter of his name is given a numeric value, the sum is 666. The author may also be thinking of a Roman coin with the emperor's image and inscription, like the one Jesus used to embarrass the Pharisees who asked about paying tribute to Caesar (see Matthew 22:15-22). For Christians, as for Jews, commerce could be problematic, involving oaths or other acknowledgments of the emperor's divinity or absolute power.

There is a striking difference between the mark of the beast and the name of the Lamb. All alike are stamped with the same impersonal number of the beast, who doesn't care who they are. But each person is called by name to follow the Lamb: Mary, favored one, the Holy Spirit will come upon you (see Luke 1:28, 35). Nathanael, Israelite without guile, I saw you under the fig tree (see John 1:47-48). Andrew, follow me and I will make you a fisher of men (see Matthew 4:19). Peter, on this rock I will build my church (see 16:18). Mary, why are you weeping? (see John 20:15-16). Saul, Saul, why are you persecuting me? (see Acts 9:4). Rather than losing our identity, each of us becomes more ourselves as we conform ourselves to Christ.

Every time you enter God's house, you retrace on your body the mark of the Lamb, by which you were permanently sealed in baptism. Does this mark effectively shape your life when you leave Mass? Just as catechumens are marked with the sign of the cross on all their limbs and senses, Christ longs for every facet of your being to bear his imprint.

What thoughts fill your *mind?* Do you give in to worry, jealousy, or unforgiveness, or do you bring these thoughts captive to Christ (see 2 Corinthians 10:5) and put on his mind instead?

What images fill your *vision*? Are you discouraged by grotesque glimpses of evil, or does your faith see and carry forward the good that God is bringing out of difficult circumstances? Do you look intently for other people's sins and missteps, or can you discern and foster the good in other people?

What words escape your *mouth*? Are they words of cursing, whining, and criticizing, or words of praise, encouragement, and comfort (see Ephesians 4:25, 5:4)?

What loads rest on your *shoulders*? Have you resentfully taken on yourself a burden that Jesus is inviting you to share with him (see Matthew 11:28-30)? Do you shrug your shoulders and wait for someone else to take responsibility for a wrong that is within your power to address?

"Jesus, you have called me by name and invited me to bear your name and be your disciple. Release your presence within me so that I can live fully as your child, with your love flowing through everything I do."

Revelation 14:1-5

[1] Then I looked, and there was the Lamb, standing on Mount Zion! And with him were one hundred forty-four thousand who had his name and his Father's name written on their foreheads. [2] And I heard a voice from heaven like the sound of many waters and like the sound of loud thunder; the voice I heard was like the sound of harpists playing on their harps, [3] and they sing a new song before the throne and before the four living creatures and before the elders. No one could learn that song except the one hundred forty-four thousand who have been redeemed from the earth. [4] It is these who have not defiled themselves with women, for they are virgins; these

follow the Lamb wherever he goes. They have been redeemed from humankind as first fruits for God and the Lamb, [5]and in their mouth no lie was found; they are blameless.

What song is your heart singing to Jesus today? Is it a blues song of doubt or despair, or is it a song of praise and worship like the one the 144,000 sing before the throne of God (Revelation 14:3-4)? Theirs is the song of complete, utter joy at being in the presence of the victorious Lord.

Unlike the heavenly assembly, we carry in our hearts the burdens and limitations of this life. But we also carry the death and resurrection of Jesus—the very reason why the 144,000 are singing! The message of our redemption is so good that even in the midst of trials, we can know an inexplicable sense of joy deep in our hearts. When things around us are turbulent, we still can linger over the fact that God is unchanging in his love and that he delights in us.

Every day, Jesus wants to sing to you about his love and mercy. Do you listen for his song and receive its consolation and strength? How do you answer? While none of us can yet learn the song of the 144,000 (Revelation 14:3), we can listen to the Holy Spirit, unite ourselves with his pleadings (which go beyond human words), and express our hearts' yearning to be completely with Jesus. What could be a more glorious song of prayer?

If you struggle with lack of joy, ask the Spirit to examine your heart. Repent of any sin he brings to mind. Then draw close to the Lord. If you're facing a difficult situation, ask him to be there with you, and tell him you want the joy of being held safely in his hands. Jesus longs to sing to you! When voices of doubt or fear rise up and threaten to drown out his still, small voice, quiet your heart and listen for his song of love.

"Jesus, we rejoice with the 144,000 because you are the Lamb who was slain for us. Pour out on us your gift of joy, and let our hearts resonate with the songs of heaven in adoration of your wonderful love. You are our strength and our song!"

Revelation 14:6-13

6 Then I saw another angel flying in midheaven, with an eternal gospel to proclaim to those who live on the earth—to every nation and tribe and language and people. 7He said in a loud voice, "Fear God and give him glory, for the hour of his judgment has come; and worship him who made heaven and earth, the sea and the springs of water."

8 Then another angel, a second, followed, saying, "Fallen, fallen is Babylon the great! She has made all nations drink of the wine of the wrath of her fornication."

9 Then another angel, a third, followed them, crying with a loud voice, "Those who worship the beast and its image, and receive a mark on their foreheads or on their hands, 10they will also drink the wine of God's wrath, poured unmixed into the cup of his anger, and they will be tormented with fire and sulfur in the presence of the holy angels and in the presence of the Lamb. 11And the smoke of their torment goes up forever and ever. There is no rest day or night for those who worship the beast and its image and for anyone who receives the mark of its name."

12 Here is a call for the endurance of the saints, those who keep the commandments of God and hold fast to the faith of Jesus.

13 And I heard a voice from heaven saying, "Write this: Blessed are the dead who from now on die in the Lord." "Yes," says the Spirit, "they will rest from their labors, for their deeds follow them."

Are you ready for a little rest and relaxation? This reading contrasts two sets of people: those who have "no rest" from torment, and those who "rest from their labors" in the presence of the Lord (Revelation 14:11, 13).

The restless people are the ones who made the disastrous choice to build their lives around something less than the God of the universe, the only proper object of worship. They are tormented by unremitting guilt because they refuse to believe the good news of forgiveness and redemption proclaimed to all who dwell on earth (Revelation 14:6). By contrast, the author or Revelation calls his readers not only to keep the faith through perseverance and endurance but to rest from their labors as well. And why rest? Because God's decisive victory is assured (14:12, 13).

We who labor in the vineyard often find it difficult to enter into the rest that God wants all of his children to enjoy. We are tormented by second-guessing our choices, wondering if we could have done a more thorough job, spoken more boldly, held our temper longer. We are discouraged by our ineffectiveness not only in turning the tide of evil in the world but in remaining faithful to the simple tasks of seeking the Lord in prayer; speaking the truth; and loving our spouse, parent, child, or co-worker.

When we give in to discouragement, it is often because we have become confused about whose work it is to build the kingdom. Although we know that only God can change hearts and overcome evil, we often think and act as if this monumental mission were entirely dependent on our efforts. No wonder we grow weary!

Jesus instead invites us to come to him and find rest, not by taking a break from our work but by uniting our efforts with his (Matthew 11:28-30). He reminds us that his Holy Spirit is at work within us to accomplish his will (Ephesians 2:10; 3:20; Philippians 2:13). The final outcome depends entirely on him and may not match what we currently observe with our limited human vision.

"Lord, I so often grow weary of doing your work. Reveal the pride that lies at the root of my discouragement. Revive my faith in your power to conquer evil, not only the evil that seems to rule the world but also the evil that lurks in my own heart. Because you love me so much, renew the strength with which I cling to your love."

Revelation 14:14-20

[14] Then I looked, and there was a white cloud, and seated on the cloud was one like the Son of Man, with a golden crown on his head, and a sharp sickle in his hand! [15]Another angel came out of the temple, calling with a loud voice to the one who sat on the cloud, "Use your sickle and reap, for the hour to reap has come, because the harvest of the earth is fully ripe." [16]So the one who sat on the cloud swung his sickle over the earth, and the earth was reaped.

[17] Then another angel came out of the temple in heaven, and he too had a sharp sickle. [18]Then another angel came out from the altar, the angel who has authority over fire, and he called with a loud voice to him who had the sharp sickle, "Use your sharp sickle and gather the clusters of the vine of the earth, for its grapes are ripe." [19]So the angel swung his sickle over the earth and gathered the vintage of the earth, and he threw it into the great wine press of the wrath of God. [20]And the wine press was trodden outside the city, and blood flowed from the wine press, as high as a horse's bridle, for a distance of about two hundred miles.

Strange and bizarre as the apocalyptic images of the book of Revelation can seem, they are intimately connected with Old Testament prophetic tradition as well as with Jesus' own parables. The prophet Joel proclaimed that Yahweh would judge the nations like those reaping crops with a sickle (see Joel 3:13). Isaiah, too, spoke of a messianic figure of judgment whose garments would be stained crimson from treading the grapes in the winepress of Yahweh's anger (see Isaiah 63:1-3).

Both prophecies parallel John's vision in Revelation: "So the angel swung his sickle on the earth and gathered the vintage of the earth, and he threw it into the great wine press of the wrath of God" (Revelation 14:19). Jesus also compared the end times to a harvest, and applied this image even more urgently. He saw beyond history, to the time when the Father would achieve his final victory: "Look around you, and see how the fields are ripe for harvesting" (John 4:35).

The "harvest" represents the culmination of a long, well-ordered progression. First the soil had to be tilled, then seeds planted, and then the fields watered and carefully tended. Only when the crop was fully mature was everything ready for the reaper. In this sequence, the inspired authors detected a ready-made symbol of God's hand guiding history. Just as a farmer prepares for the faraway—but inevitable—harvest, so God was constantly preparing people for the end of history.

Only by faith can we believe that the world will end, not through some meaningless cataclysm, but through the full establishment of the kingdom of God. The process has already begun. Though we struggle with evil, every day we draw closer to Christ's triumphant return. Revelation reminds us that we are to be every bit as sure of God's eventual victory as the farmer is sure of the coming harvest.

Jesus invited us to participate actively in the harvest: "Ask the Lord of the harvest to send out laborers into his harvest" (Matthew 9:38). Let us ask God to give us the grace to work with him as he gathers "fruit for eternal life" (John 4:36).

"Father, we pray for all of those you would gather into your church. By your Spirit, help us to be faithful servants who prepare the way for the return of your Son, Jesus Christ."

Revelation 15:1-4

[1] Then I saw another portent in heaven, great and amazing: seven angels with seven plagues, which are the last, for with them the wrath of God is ended.

[2] And I saw what appeared to be a sea of glass mixed with fire, and those who had conquered the beast and its image and the number of its name, standing beside the sea of glass with harps of God in their hands. [3]And they sing the song of Moses, the servant of God, and the song of the Lamb:

"Great and amazing are your deeds,
　　Lord God the Almighty!
Just and true are your ways,
　　King of the nations!
[4] Lord, who will not fear
　　and glorify your name?
For you alone are holy.
　　All nations will come
　　and worship before you,
for your judgments have been revealed."

Heavenly Father, open our eyes to see what the saints in heaven see. May we behold your beauty and be overwhelmed by your love.

"Show us your glory in ways that we cannot even imagine. We want to join the church triumphant in singing the song of Moses and the song of the Lamb. You have done great and marvelous things!

"Almighty God, you are love itself, and out of love, you made all things. Our hearts are stirred when we consider that with a word, you created the heavens and the earth. It was easy for you to create all the trees of the field and every living thing with your own hands. Who can fathom your greatness? As we consider that you fashioned the majestic mountains and formed the vast seas, and when we contemplate that you stretched out your hand and the boundless universe was made, we are left speechless. Nothing is too difficult for you! No force in heaven or on earth could ever oppose you.

"God our Father, you made us as your most treasured possession, and promised your faithfulness to all generations. Even when we sinned again and again, you did not turn away from us, as we deserved. No, you faithfully pursued your children in every generation! In the fullness of time, you showed us the depth of your love when you sent us your only Son, Jesus, born of a woman, to die in our place and save us from sin and death. How much you must love us! We cannot help but praise and worship you!

"O Lord, our God, how can we be silent when we consider who you are, and all your deeds? Your great love for us causes us to bow down in worship and adoration. Who will not fear you, O Lord? You are awesome—ever worthy of praise. How can we not bring glory to your name? You love is so wonderful that we want to glorify you both now and forever!

"Father, fill your kingdom to overflowing! Send your Holy Spirit into the world today to reveal your glory to all people! May all men and women acknowledge your holiness! May every person—from great and famous kings and queens to the meekest and the lowliest—experience your great love, Lord. Let all creation give you praise and honor and glory!"

Seven Bowls and the Fall of Babylon

Revelation 15:5–19:10

Seven Bowls and the Fall of Babylon
Revelation 15:5–19:10

Revelation 15:5-8

5 After this I looked, and the temple of the tent of witness in heaven was opened, 6and out of the temple came the seven angels with the seven plagues, robed in pure bright linen, with golden sashes across their chests. 7Then one of the four living creatures gave the seven angels seven golden bowls full of the wrath of God, who lives forever and ever; 8and the temple was filled with smoke from the glory of God and from his power, and no one could enter the temple until the seven plagues of the seven angels were ended.

Because Christianity is founded on the miracle of the incarnation—the Word becoming flesh—the idea of God's presence is not abstract, something to be grasped only through intellectual effort. Rather, God draws near to us through our senses, as well. And that's why this passage from Revelation is so gripping. Its description of God's heavenly temple is full of sensory images. The angels wear pure white linen and shiny golden belts. The temple is so filled with "smoke from the glory of God and from his power" that there is no room for anyone to enter.

These images deliberately recall God's dwelling places in the Old Testament—from the tent in the desert to the glorious temple of Solomon. Before Moses erected the tabernacle, God's presence as cloud by day and fire by night preceded the people on their journey. When they saw that cloud, they knew that their leader had entered into communion with God (see Exodus 33:9-11). In the desert tabernacle, all the vessels were of gleaming gold (see 37), and the presence of God filled the dwelling as a smoky cloud (see 40:34).

Solomon used precious metals for the vessels in the temple (see 1 Kings 7:48-50), and God showed his favor by entering that temple in a glorious cloud (see 8:10-11), which again left the ministers unable to enter.

From exile in Babylon, Ezekiel penned a lengthy vision of a temple to replace the one Nebuchadnezzar had destroyed. Again, God's glory filled the temple (see Ezekiel 43:2-4), this time with the sound of rushing waters. After the people returned from exile, the temple that they rebuilt hardly matched its former glory, but Sirach described worship there with idealized images of glory and fire (see Sirach 50:5-11). Cleansing and rededicating the temple was essential for the Maccabees (see 1 Maccabees 4:42-59), and the miracle of the sanctuary lights has persevered in the celebration of Hanukkah.

Gold, smoke, rushing waters—What sensory images help lift your heart? For some, it may be the lingering scent of incense; for others, a small sanctuary light in a dim chapel. Some are moved by the thundering strains of classical music like Handel's *Messiah*, while others respond to the sound of trickling water in the baptismal font. Often our hearts respond to images from nature: the first light of dawn, darting fireflies, a mountain panorama, a rainbow-crowned waterfall. The taste of an ethnic holiday food or the texture of a handmade tablecloth or baptismal garment may stir grateful memories.

If you customarily pray only with a Bible, try enhancing your worship by adding a sensory object: light a candle, play instrumental music, gaze on an icon, use incense, hold a rough wooden cross in your hands, or slowly read the day's psalm aloud. Don't be afraid to let your body and feelings respond to God's presence. This is a concrete way to join the worship continually being offered at the heavenly altar!

"God Almighty, you fill the universe, yet you choose to dwell in my humanity. Make me more responsive to your presence."

Revelation 16:1-11

¹ Then I heard a loud voice from the temple telling the seven angels, "Go and pour out on the earth the seven bowls of the wrath of God."

² So the first angel went and poured his bowl on the earth, and a foul and painful sore came on those who had the mark of the beast and who worshiped its image.

³ The second angel poured his bowl into the sea, and it became like the blood of a corpse, and every living thing in the sea died.

⁴ The third angel poured his bowl into the rivers and the springs of water, and they became blood. ⁵And I heard the angel of the waters say,

"You are just, O Holy One, who are and were,
for you have judged these things;
⁶ because they shed the blood of
saints and prophets,
you have given them blood to drink.
It is what they deserve!"

⁷And I heard the altar respond,

"Yes, O Lord God, the Almighty,
your judgments are true and just!"

⁸ The fourth angel poured his bowl on the sun, and it was allowed to scorch people with fire; ⁹they were scorched by the fierce heat, but they cursed the name of God, who had authority over these plagues, and they did not repent and give him glory.

¹⁰ The fifth angel poured his bowl on the throne of the beast, and its kingdom was plunged into darkness; people gnawed their tongues in agony, ¹¹and cursed the God of heaven because of their pains and sores, and they did not repent of their deeds.

Faced with God's judgment, human beings have a clear choice: remain on the path of death, or find the way of repentance that leads to life. Again and again Revelation sounds this sad refrain: "[They] cursed the God of heaven because of their pains and sores, and they did not repent of their deeds" (Revelation 16:11). Like small children called to clean up the mess they have made, they are quick to blame each other—and slow to take responsibility for the task of restoration.

God's judgment is just and fitting. Those who worship the grotesque image of the beast are themselves disfigured by foul sores that externally manifest the way they have steeped their minds and feelings in evil schemes and desires (Revelation 16:2). In contrast, a wise wag advises us to practice smiling so that as we age, our inevitable wrinkles will be in the right places.

The natural consequence of living by violence and bloodshed is to become a victim of violence oneself (Revelation 16:6). This is the final result of a dehumanizing transformation that begins when a person nurtures resentment and hatred until it crowds out any possibility of love and forgiveness.

Those who do not come to the lamp God holds up to show the way of repentance are seared by the unrelenting light that exposes their evil deeds (Revelation 16:8). If we hide behind half-truths, we will find it increasingly difficult to recognize and profess the full truth that sets us free.

Those who act on the impulses from their shadow side wind up stumbling in total darkness (Revelation 16:10). The evil they turned against others winds up destroying them.

All these plagues, reminiscent of the plagues that preceded the Exodus, have the effect of hardening God's enemies in their rebellion—and opening a way of escape for God's chosen people. Finding that way, however, requires humility and confidence in the judge who is also our redeemer. "When these things begin to take place," counsels Jesus, "stand up and raise your heads, because your redemption is drawing near" (Luke 21:28).

We, too, have a clear choice in the face of natural disasters, unforeseen reversals of fortune, or crushing disappointments. We can blame and rail against God, digging ourselves deeper and deeper into resentment, anger, and hatred. Or, we can seek God's hand in the midst of these circumstances, bringing us up short with a warning, indicating a shift in emphasis or direction, inviting us to trust more explicitly in his loving providence. The choice is ours.

"You are justified, Lord, when you condemn. I am in no way deserving of your forgiveness, and yet you offer it to me again and again. Help me trace the rainbow through the rain, cling to your promise, and set out on the path you set before me."

Revelation 16:12-21

[12] The sixth angel poured his bowl on the great river Euphrates, and its water was dried up in order to prepare the way for the kings from the east. [13]And I saw three foul spirits like frogs coming from the mouth of the dragon, from the mouth of the beast, and from the mouth of the false prophet. [14]These are demonic spirits, performing signs, who go abroad to the kings of the whole world, to assemble them for battle on the great day of God the Almighty. [15] ("See, I am coming like a thief! Blessed is the one who stays awake and is clothed, not going about naked and exposed to shame.") [16]And they assembled them at the place that in Hebrew is called Harmagedon. [17] The seventh angel poured his bowl into the air, and a loud voice came out of the temple, from the throne, saying, "It is done!" [18]And there came flashes of lightning, rumblings, peals of thunder, and a violent earthquake, such as had not occurred since people were

upon the earth, so violent was that earthquake. [19]The great city was split into three parts, and the cities of the nations fell. God remembered great Babylon and gave her the wine-cup of the fury of his wrath. [20]And every island fled away, and no mountains were to be found; [21]and huge hailstones, each weighing about a hundred pounds, dropped from heaven on people, until they cursed God for the plague of the hail, so fearful was that plague.

I t is done!" declares the voice from the temple. The accompanying signs are powerful: lightning, thunder, earthquake, hailstones.

"It is finished!" cries Jesus from the cross, his pulpit and throne (John 19:30). Here, too, there are clear signs: darkness, earthquakes, split rocks, opened tombs (see Matthew 27:45, 51-52). These signs proclaim a single message: God is on the move!

Finished. The price of our salvation has been paid. Punishment for all the sins of humankind has been heaped on the willing victim. He has gone down to the realm of death bearing the keys of liberation so that no one needs to be imprisoned in eternal death. He has decisively defeated our enemy and God's. The victor is on the move to establish his kingdom once and for all.

Finished. Yet not over. The followers of Jesus will spread the good news of salvation throughout the earth, yet many of them will be put to death like their master. The church, his people on earth, will be torn by division, plagued by scandal, disfigured by sin. Deadly hostile forces, inimical to the gospel, will swell until they seem to control the whole earth. The worldly and demonic forces of evil are being assembled at Armageddon.

And yet there is no doubt about the outcome of this contest! It has already been decided on the hill of Calvary. The moment that seemed like the final triumph of evil provided the gateway to the victory of life over death, light over darkness, love over hatred.

Do we dare believe this proclamation? Can we live in quiet

confidence that God is in the process of establishing his kingdom on earth? Can we turn a deaf ear to the siren call of the world, the flesh, and the devil and take our marching orders instead from Christ, victim and victor? Come to him for direction. Where would he have you stand? Which breaches would he have you repair? Where is the next skirmish involving you, one part of the great battle plan that is known to him alone?

Christians who enjoy assurance of Christ's victory can sing a song of victory in the midst of defeat. Listen to Paul and Silas, whose hymns in prison awakened the earthquake that set them free and opened the way of salvation for their jailer and his entire family (see Acts 16:25-34). Listen to the countless martyrs of more recent times, singing "We Shall Overcome" in the most difficult circumstances.

"Jesus Christ, risen from the dead, you have defeated sin and all the powers of evil! I rejoice in the salvation you have accomplished and long to see it fully achieved on earth."

Revelation 17:1-8

[1] Then one of the seven angels who had the seven bowls came and said to me, "Come, I will show you the judgment of the great whore who is seated on many waters, [2]with whom the kings of the earth have committed fornication, and with the wine of whose fornication the inhabitants of the earth have become drunk." [3]So he carried me away in the spirit into a wilderness, and I saw a woman sitting on a scarlet beast that was full of blasphemous names, and it had seven heads and ten horns. [4]The woman was clothed in purple and scarlet, and adorned with gold and jewels and pearls, holding in her hand a golden cup full of abominations and the impurities of her fornication; [5]and on her forehead was written a name, a mystery:

"Babylon the great, mother of whores and of earth's abominations." [6]And I saw that the woman was drunk with the blood of the saints and the blood of the witnesses to Jesus.

When I saw her, I was greatly amazed. [7]But the angel said to me, "Why are you so amazed? I will tell you the mystery of the woman, and of the beast with seven heads and ten horns that carries her. [8]The beast that you saw was, and is not, and is about to ascend from the bottomless pit and go to destruction. And the inhabitants of the earth, whose names have not been written in the book of life from the foundation of the world, will be amazed when they see the beast, because it was and is not and is to come.

In contrast to the woman of God in Revelation 12, which we may read both as Mary and as the church, we have here a fascinating picture of "Babylon," the great harlot, mother and source of all evil. Although she is arrayed in the colors of royalty and power, those titles are blasphemous, usurping power that belongs to God alone. The golden cup that she holds is full of abominations and impurities, and she is intoxicated with the blood of the Christians she has put to death.

The author of Revelation is using these images to refer to Rome, the world power occupying the place Babylon had held seven centuries earlier. His meaning is clear, but he dare not name the power that is still ruling his world. He condemns Rome for her licentiousness, her idolatry, her claim to possess ultimate power, and for the violence and economic injustice with which she imposed her rule over the whole world.

The historic Babylon served as the instrument of God's judgment on the nation of Judah, which had forsaken him to follow other gods and seek security in military alliances (see Isaiah 39:6). Babylon was responsible for destroying the city of Jerusalem and its temple and carrying its citizens into exile. Yet, the prophets also declare God's judgment on Babylon for her many sins and crimes (see 47:1-9).

This is certainly a graphic picture, but the writer cautions us not to get bogged down in the details of the portrait. "Why are you so amazed?" asks the angel (Revelation 17:7) Leave wonder and speculation to those whose names are not written in the Lamb's book of life. The exact nature of this woman's fornications is immaterial; it is sufficient to know that she has led many people into idolatry, that she has made war on the holy people of God. We shouldn't be surprised that she stands under God's judgment. And neither should we be preoccupied with the way in which that judgment will fall.

God is King of Kings and Lord of Lords. He can marshal any human or heavenly power to carry out his will. Just as he used the armies of Rome to bring judgment on the Jewish leaders who rejected Jesus' message of salvation, he can use barbarian hordes to bring down the Roman Empire, all in his good time. Christians should be careful not to place all our hope in—or become too frightened of—secular powers. After all, we serve a King who rules in justice and mercy. He will triumph over every form of evil and corruption, whether that be in our government, in our neighborhood, or even in the secrecy of our own hearts!

"Lord, help me to focus my attention in the right place, not to flirt with evil by becoming fascinated with it, but to keep my eyes fixed on the pattern of life and holiness you offer me."

Revelation 17:9-18

9 "This calls for a mind that has wisdom: the seven heads are seven mountains on which the woman is seated; also, they are seven kings, 10 of whom five have fallen, one is living, and the other has not yet

come; and when he comes, he must remain only a little while. [11]As for the beast that was and is not, it is an eighth but it belongs to the seven, and it goes to destruction. [12]And the ten horns that you saw are ten kings who have not yet received a kingdom, but they are to receive authority as kings for one hour, together with the beast. [13]These are united in yielding their power and authority to the beast; [14]they will make war on the Lamb, and the Lamb will conquer them, for he is Lord of lords and King of kings, and those with him are called and chosen and faithful."

[15] And he said to me, "The waters that you saw, where the whore is seated, are peoples and multitudes and nations and languages. [16]And the ten horns that you saw, they and the beast will hate the whore; they will make her desolate and naked; they will devour her flesh and burn her up with fire. [17]For God has put it into their hearts to carry out his purpose by agreeing to give their kingdom to the beast, until the words of God will be fulfilled. [18]The woman you saw is the great city that rules over the kings of the earth."

If there remains any doubt that John is talking about Rome, these verses should dispel it. John refers to the proverbial seven hills (Revelation 17:9). He even mentions a succession of kings, which may be identified as some of the emperors who made life most difficult for Christians. Still, all of these details are relatively unimportant. They fit into a clear perspective: The power of these secular rulers is limited! It lasts "for one hour" (17:12). Their persecution of the people of God is real and fierce, but God will raise up "peoples and multitudes and nations and tongues" who hate Rome and will destroy her.

All this occurs in fulfillment of God's eternal purposes. He alone is King of Kings and Lord of Lords, and he "has put it into their hearts to carry out his purpose," just as earlier he used Assyria as the rod of his anger (see Isaiah 10:5), Babylon to punish his people, and the

Persian Cyrus (called God's "anointed" in Isaiah 45:1-6, though he does not even acknowledge God!) to liberate the Jews from exile.

Nothing that happens on earth is outside divine providence. This message must have been a great comfort to Christians who were being forced to witness the martyrdom of their fellow believers. Through the vicissitudes of successive emperors and military commanders, they might have to lay their lives on the line, but they could be confident that God was in charge.

From the fact that Jesus is King of Kings and Lord of Lords, his followers also receive their unchanging identity: "Those with him are called and chosen and faithful" (Revelation 17:14).

"Called by name," our own individual names and the name "Christian," called to follow the Lamb wherever he goes, united with him in love, beloved sons and daughters of his Father, filled with the Holy Spirit that shaped his impulses and choices.

"Chosen" as he chose a people long ago to receive the revelation of who God is and how he made us to live in community with him and each other. Set apart for his loving purpose, hand-selected and formed through the experiences and relationships of our lives.

"Faithful" in response to the fidelity of the one who is incapable of denying himself (see 2 Timothy 2:13) and his image in us. Loyal because he is extravagantly committed to our well-being. Keeping the faith entrusted to us by those who have gone before us marked with the sign of faith.

More important, however, than being "called, chosen, and faithful" is what comes first: "those with him." We are united with the King of Kings and Lord of Lords! What more could we ask or imagine?

"King of Kings, Lord of Lords, all times and events are in your hands. Thank you for uniting yourself to me through my baptism. Let your courage and your love live in me."

Revelation 18:1-8

[1] After this I saw another angel coming down from heaven, having great authority; and the earth was made bright with his splendor.
[2]He called out with a mighty voice,
    "Fallen, fallen is Babylon the great!
        It has become a dwelling place of demons,
    a haunt of every foul spirit,
        a haunt of every foul bird,
        a haunt of every foul and hateful beast.
[3] For all the nations have drunk
        of the wine of the wrath of her fornication,
    and the kings of the earth have
            committed fornication with her,
        and the merchants of the earth
            have grown rich from the power of her luxury."
[4] Then I heard another voice from heaven saying,
    "Come out of her, my people,
        so that you do not take part in her sins,
    and so that you do not share in her plagues;
[5] for her sins are heaped high as heaven,
        and God has remembered her iniquities.
[6] Render to her as she herself has rendered,
        and repay her double for her deeds;
        mix a double draught for her in the cup she mixed.
[7] As she glorified herself and lived luxuriously,
        so give her a like measure of torment and grief.
    Since in her heart she says,
        'I rule as a queen;
    I am no widow,
        and I will never see grief,'
[8] therefore her plagues will come in a single day—
        pestilence and mourning and famine—

and she will be burned with fire;
for mighty is the Lord God who judges her."

Believing in Jesus cost the early churches dearly. It seemed unjust that Christians should lose everything when Almighty God was on their side!

The prophetic exhortations recorded in Revelation helped to answer the first Christians' questions about why God did not immediately step in to save them. John reassured them that they had not been forgotten. One day, they would see evil destroyed in the most swift, decisive, and one-sided battle of all time. All the martyrs of every age will be vindicated, and God's salvation will win out over the emptiness of the world's fleeting pleasures.

Throughout Revelation, "Babylon the great" symbolized not only the Roman empire, but the entire world system that has set itself against the reign of God. One day, the world will be judged according to God's will for creation, and an end will come to all the debates and opinions of right and wrong, moral and immoral. On that day, it will be made clear that all of God's "judgments are true and just" (Revelation 19:2).

In Revelation, the sin in the world is called "fornication" because of the way worldly things can entice people away from God. When the pursuit of pleasure becomes people's dominant goal, God's beauty and salvation are veiled. As a result, people are robbed of their hope of redemption.

Revelation warns us to be alert to the influence of evil. Through the media, we are constantly enticed to live for ourselves and to accept ungodliness from a world that is increasingly anti-Christian. To counter this, we should fix our hearts on the beauty of Christ and boldly speak out about his greatness. God wants us to distance ourselves from the allure of the world and to embrace his salvation. As we draw nearer to the Lord, praise will erupt from our hearts.

We will join with the heavenly hosts singing, "Salvation and glory and power to our God" (Revelation 19:1). Let us rejoice today in our assurance that God will ultimately triumph over every power opposed to him.

"Thank you, Father, for inviting me to the wedding banquet of the Lamb. I eagerly await the day that you overthrow evil. Until that day, I will take my stand with you in confidence, knowing that the victory is yours."

Revelation 18:9-20

9 And the kings of the earth, who committed fornication and lived in luxury with her, will weep and wail over her when they see the smoke of her burning; [10]they will stand far off, in fear of her torment, and say,

"Alas, alas, the great city,
    Babylon, the mighty city!
For in one hour your judgment has come."

11 And the merchants of the earth weep and mourn for her, since no one buys their cargo anymore, [12]cargo of gold, silver, jewels and pearls, fine linen, purple, silk and scarlet, all kinds of scented wood, all articles of ivory, all articles of costly wood, bronze, iron, and marble, [13]cinnamon, spice, incense, myrrh, frankincense, wine, olive oil, choice flour and wheat, cattle and sheep, horses and chariots, slaves—and human lives.

14 "The fruit for which your soul longed
        has gone from you,
    and all your dainties and your splendor
        are lost to you,
        never to be found again!"

15 The merchants of these wares, who gained wealth from her, will

stand far off, in fear of her torment, weeping and mourning aloud, ¹⁶ "Alas, alas, the great city,

> clothed in fine linen,
>> in purple and scarlet,
> adorned with gold,
>> with jewels, and with pearls!

¹⁷ For in one hour all this wealth has been laid waste!"

And all shipmasters and seafarers, sailors and all whose trade is on the sea, stood far off ¹⁸and cried out as they saw the smoke of her burning,

> "What city was like the great city?"

¹⁹And they threw dust on their heads, as they wept and mourned, crying out,

> "Alas, alas, the great city,
>> where all who had ships at sea
>> grew rich by her wealth!
> For in one hour she has been laid waste.

²⁰ Rejoice over her, O heaven,
>> you saints and apostles and prophets!
> For God has given judgment for you against her."

G reed shows itself in many ways. We see it when corporate executives try to swindle investors; when landlords ask for exorbitant rents that only the very rich can afford; or when doctors deliberately overcharge their indigent patients. We see it when holiday shoppers push, shove, and even trample other customers to get to those "must-have" items. But mostly, greed shows itself in unhappiness. Those who are caught up in greed really can't be happy, because they can never have enough.

Greed is really the mind-set of the "kings of the earth" and the merchants who are lamenting the downfall of Babylon here. They're not upset about the destruction of Babylon; as one translation tells us, they are watching from a "safe distance" so that they won't get hurt. No, their "weeping and wailing" is not over the sad turn of events that Babylon must suffer. It is over the fact that they can no longer make a profit from her! Most likely, they are pretty well-off materially, but they are still upset because they can't acquire more, and they somehow think that doing so will bring them peace of mind.

Contrast the misery of the greedy with the attitude the apostles are told to have: They are not to weep over the destruction of Babylon; on the contrary, they are to rejoice over it (Revelation 18:20)! This rejoicing is not meant to be some kind of gloating over the destruction of an earthly city. Rather, they are to be happy because the darkness that Babylon represents has no more power over humankind. All the structures of sin that have exploited and enslaved humanity for centuries have been torn down. What other response could there be but joyful celebration?

The question for us is, How can I keep my eyes on this vision of future glory? We must have possessions, but we don't want to spend our lives running after them. So often, when we should be filled with the peace of the Lord, we are preoccupied instead with the worries of the world. Jesus didn't come to deliver us from our problems, but he did come to give us real, abiding joy, "a garland instead of ashes, the oil of gladness instead of mourning, the mantle of praise instead of a faint spirit" (Isaiah 61:3).

Are you busy thinking about how you'll get by tomorrow, or about the things you don't have? Then just spend some time thanking God for what you do have—the love of Christ, poured into your heart by the Holy Spirit. He is truly the greatest treasure you can possess!

"Lord, I want to live a life of radical joy. I give my anxieties and burdens to you. Help me to rise above them to live constantly in your presence."

Revelation 18:21-24

²¹ Then a mighty angel took up a stone like a great millstone and threw it into the sea, saying,

"With such violence Babylon the great city
  will be thrown down,
    and will be found no more;
²² and the sound of harpists and minstrels and of flutists
      and trumpeters
    will be heard in you no more;
and an artisan of any trade
    will be found in you no more;
and the sound of the millstone
    will be heard in you no more;
²³ and the light of a lamp
    will shine in you no more;
and the voice of bridegroom and bride
    will be heard in you no more;
for your merchants were the magnates of the earth,
    and all nations were deceived by your sorcery.
²⁴ And in you was found the blood of prophets and of saints,
    and of all who have been slaughtered on earth."

Reading this description of Babylon's destruction, we are left speechless. If there was ever a picture of desolation, this is it. There is no more music, no more culture, no more industry, and the institution of marriage has disintegrated. All the things that we associate with a thriving society have disappeared, and the angel says they are never to return. Never? That's a hard word to hear; over and over again, the Bible tells us about the mercy of God. Why would he punish any nation so severely? Is our God really so full of wrath and vengeance?

The answer is a resounding, "No!" We know that God *is* loving and merciful, and that he wants no one to be condemned but desires all to "come to repentance." (2 Peter 3:9). However, he cannot force us to accept his love; the choice is up to us. We have the freedom to reject his grace, but when we do, we get ourselves into trouble. We have only to look around the world to see the fruits of that choice: rampant poverty, crime, divorce, and so many other ills that can bring about a culture of death, instead of the abundant life Jesus wants for all his people.

Babylon is certainly guilty of sin, and even worse, of seducing the whole world to go along with it. The great millstone (see Revelation 18:21) reminds us of Jesus' parable: if we lead others to sin, it would be better if we were thrown into the sea with a millstone around our necks (see Mark 9:42). But the biggest problem is not Babylon's sin—it's that Babylon has denied *God's remedy* for sin, by shedding the blood of the prophets and saints who announced his salvation (see Revelation 18:24). The resulting destruction is not really God's doing; it's what happens whenever man decides that he simply won't listen to the still, small voice of the Holy Spirit speaking to his heart.

As unsettling as the angel's pronouncements may be, they should remind us of how much we need God's mercy and blessings—and of our calling to share them with those who are lost. If we look around us, we will surely find some "desolate" places that are thirsting for his refreshing presence: Is our home filled with peace, or is it marked by tension and hostility? Do we bring the Holy Spirit to our workplaces, or do we go along with gossip, office politics, and the "bottom-line" mentality? We have the chance to bring his living water into our desert situations, and to make them come alive with his love!

"Lord, bring all of your children out of the desert and into new life. Transform our hearts, our homes, and our communities by the power of your Spirit!"

Revelation 19:1-10

[1] After this I heard what seemed to be the loud voice of a great multitude in heaven, saying,
"Hallelujah!
Salvation and glory and power to our God,
[2]   for his judgments are true and just;
he has judged the great whore
    who corrupted the earth with her fornication,
and he has avenged on her the blood of his servants."
[3]Once more they said,
"Hallelujah!
The smoke goes up from her forever and ever."
[4]And the twenty-four elders and the four living creatures fell down and worshiped God who is seated on the throne, saying,
"Amen. Hallelujah!"
[5] And from the throne came a voice saying,
"Praise our God,
    all you his servants,
and all who fear him,
    small and great."
[6] Then I heard what seemed to be the voice of a great multitude, like the sound of many waters and like the sound of mighty thunder-peals, crying out,
"Hallelujah!
For the Lord our God
    the Almighty reigns.
[7] Let us rejoice and exult
    and give him the glory,
for the marriage of the Lamb has come,
    and his bride has made herself ready;
[8] to her it has been granted to be clothed

with fine linen, bright and pure"—
for the fine linen is the righteous deeds of the saints.
⁹ And the angel said to me, "Write this: Blessed are those who are invited to the marriage supper of the Lamb." And he said to me, "These are true words of God." ¹⁰Then I fell down at his feet to worship him, but he said to me, "You must not do that! I am a fellow servant with you and your comrades who hold the testimony of Jesus. Worship God! For the testimony of Jesus is the spirit of prophecy."

How would you feel if you were a part of this great multitude? Obviously, you'd be saying to yourself, "What an incredible occasion!" All the celebrations you had attended during your earthly life would be nothing compared to this. For this crowd is cheering the fact that your mortal enemy, Satan, is no more. All of the devastation caused by sin, and all the havoc wreaked by the "principalities and powers" has been undone. The battle is over, and the festivities will continue for all eternity!

But while you might be contemplating how joyful you'll be in heaven praising God with all the saints, don't forget about how much joy *heaven* has over you right now! Think back for a moment to when you first came to the Lord. You may not have noticed it, but the angels were celebrating. According to Jesus' parable of the lost sheep, there can be no doubt about it: "I tell you, there will be more joy in heaven over one sinner who repents than over ninety-nine righteous persons who need no repentance" (Luke 15:7).

If we are walking in God's grace, he's very pleased with us. But he knows that we stumble, and he's even more pleased when we return to him. He is intimately aware of every move we make and every thought we think; but he's not waiting like the Pharisees, ready to trip us up every time we make a mistake. He gives us his Spirit to correct us when we fall, and when we resist temptation and grow in virtue, he's there to cheer us on—along with the "cloud of wit-nesses," the saints and angels who are praying for us!

If heaven is trying so hard to encourage us, we can be a little more encouraging to ourselves. We don't have to wait until we're at the gates of heaven to see the kind of progress we have made. Every time we hold our temper, forgive our neighbor, or restrain from over-indulgence, we have achieved something. When we endure suffering with joy, we have won another battle. When we entrust God with a difficult situation and he pulls us through it, we have grown in our faith.

The bottom line is that our spiritual life should not consist of concentrating on our failures! While we are always to remember that it's God who wins our victories, we should rejoice in them, however small, for they are fulfilling his promise to us, that "the one who began a good work among you will bring it to completion by the day of Jesus Christ" (Philippians 1:6).

"Thank you, Lord, for the gift of your grace at work in my life. Help me to see how I can do better, but also show me how far I have come. May I never forget that your Spirit is truly alive in me."

Visions of Victory and the New Jerusalem

Revelation 19:11–22:5

Visions of Victory and the New Jerusalem
Revelation 19:11–22:5

Revelation 19:11-21

[11] Then I saw heaven opened, and there was a white horse! Its rider is called Faithful and True, and in righteousness he judges and makes war. [12]His eyes are like a flame of fire, and on his head are many diadems; and he has a name inscribed that no one knows but himself. [13]He is clothed in a robe dipped in blood, and his name is called The Word of God. [14]And the armies of heaven, wearing fine linen, white and pure, were following him on white horses. [15]From his mouth comes a sharp sword with which to strike down the nations, and he will rule them with a rod of iron; he will tread the wine press of the fury of the wrath of God the Almighty. [16]On his robe and on his thigh he has a name inscribed, "King of kings and Lord of lords."

[17] Then I saw an angel standing in the sun, and with a loud voice he called to all the birds that fly in midheaven, "Come, gather for the great supper of God, [18]to eat the flesh of kings, the flesh of captains, the flesh of the mighty, the flesh of horses and their riders—flesh of all, both free and slave, both small and great." [19]Then I saw the beast and the kings of the earth with their armies gathered to make war against the rider on the horse and against his army. [20]And the beast was captured, and with it the false prophet who had performed in its presence the signs by which he deceived those who had received the mark of the beast and those who worshiped its image. These two were thrown alive into the lake of fire that burns with sulfur. [21]And the rest were killed by the sword of the rider on the horse, the sword that came from his mouth; and all the birds were gorged with their flesh. ☙

If you've ever been to Mass at a big cathedral, you may remember watching the Bible process down the aisle in the hands of the priest. However, it wasn't just carried on one arm; it was held in the air. It was rather large too, and probably enclosed in its own ornamented cover. Before the lector started to read from that Bible, incense was sprinkled around the pulpit. No doubt, seeing the word of God treated this way gave you a special sense of its power—you may have even sat up a little straighter!

Here in John's vision, we see one aspect of that power displayed even more dramatically: the power of God's word to judge between good and evil. Jesus Christ, the Word made flesh, is seated on a white horse. He is confronting the nations with their sinfulness, but consider how he does it—he speaks. The sword that comes from his mouth is the truth, and it becomes a judgment on those who have rejected it. It's a terrifying scene, but it reveals that his word is not just *about* truth; it *is* Truth!

While God's word doesn't come to us with condemnation—as his judgment does to these rebellious nations—it does have the power to shake us up. It is "living and active, sharper than any two-edged sword." It can divide "soul from spirit, joints from marrow; it is able to judge the thoughts and intentions of the heart" (Hebrews 4:12). We have all had times when we have felt God's word touching those places that need our attention—areas of unforgiveness, anger, lust, or pride. We might even call it "God's X-ray machine," because it always sees right through us!

When we are convicted by the word of God, it may hurt a little bit as we realize how far we still have to go on the road to holiness. But unlike the criticism the world dishes out, God's word carries with it the love of the Holy Spirit, prompting us to change our ways and also giving us the grace to do so. We can be thankful that the Scriptures work not only to take us away from sin, but to bring us new life. Truly, they are the "imperishable seed" that can help lead us to heaven (1 Peter 1:23)!

"Father, thank you for the table of your word! Give me a hunger to feast on its nourishment, and send me the fire of your Spirit that I may be conformed to the living Word, Jesus Christ. May the Scriptures penetrate my heart and change my life!"

Revelation 20:1-6

[1] Then I saw an angel coming down from heaven, holding in his hand the key to the bottomless pit and a great chain. [2]He seized the dragon, that ancient serpent, who is the Devil and Satan, and bound him for a thousand years, [3]and threw him into the pit, and locked and sealed it over him, so that he would deceive the nations no more, until the thousand years were ended. After that he must be let out for a little while.
[4] Then I saw thrones, and those seated on them were given authority to judge. I also saw the souls of those who had been beheaded for their testimony to Jesus and for the word of God. They had not worshiped the beast or its image and had not received its mark on their foreheads or their hands. They came to life and reigned with Christ a thousand years. [5](The rest of the dead did not come to life until the thousand years were ended.) This is the first resurrection. [6]Blessed and holy are those who share in the first resurrection. Over these the second death has no power, but they will be priests of God and of Christ, and they will reign with him a thousand years.

The Book of Revelation is often perceived as predictions of future events, and can conjure up fear in its readers. Many would-be interpreters have speculated about which contemporary world leaders were represented by certain passages in the book. When prayerfully read and carefully studied, the book of Revelation is actually a prophetic word of encouragement to a people undergoing persecution. From this perspective, the book is a lot more relevant to our lives than if it were a predictor of specific events.

Revelation consistently makes the point that through Jesus Christ, God has given us complete victory over Satan, sin, and death. By the power of the Spirit, this victorious God dwells in us, and this should make us joyful. Judgment will come, and Satan's condemnation will be certain. For those who turn from sin and accept the redemption that God has given us in Jesus, there will be mercy.

As we pray for ourselves and others, we can be filled with hope that God will not only show his mercy, but will bless us with everything he has planned for us since the beginning of time. We who trust in God are the bride, chosen for Jesus by the Father. As his bride, we can approach him with complete confidence that he will bring us into his Father's house, not just as servants—nor even just as friends—but as those he has chosen to be his very own.

As we read the Book of Revelation, we can't help but feel that we are moving closer to the summing up of all of God's intentions. As we wait for his return, and for the fulfillment of all God has planned, we can continually receive more and more from the Lord by turning to him each day. God's marvelous light will penetrate the deepest places to bring us healing. Fear and doubt will be swept aside as we come to know our Lord and Savior more and more intimately.

"Father, we want to love you and to love your people. Help us to fix our hearts and minds on the fulfillment of your plan, when we, your bride, will finally be united with you, our bridegroom. Through your word, comfort our hearts and the hearts of Christians everywhere with your love and mercy."

Revelation 20:7-10

7 When the thousand years are ended, Satan will be released from his prison 8and will come out to deceive the nations at the four corners of the earth, Gog and Magog, in order to gather them for battle; they are as numerous as the sands of the sea. 9They marched up over the breadth of the earth and surrounded the camp of the saints and the beloved city. And fire came down from heaven and consumed them. 10And the devil who had deceived them was thrown into the lake of fire and sulfur, where the beast and the false prophet were, and they will be tormented day and night forever and ever.

If Revelation were written like a spy thriller, Satan would play the despicable and crafty villain who is planning to dominate the entire world by going out to "deceive the nations." While he thinks he has arranged a decisive confrontation between his followers and "the good guys," it's only because someone else is pulling the strings. It was God who let him out of his prison in the first place. According to the way Revelation describes him, Satan is truly powerless; he is no more than a "fall guy" who has been set up to bring about God's victory!

Our catechism tells us, "It is a great mystery that providence should permit diabolical activity," but also reminds us: "In everything God works for good with those who love him" (*Catechism of the Catholic Church*, 395). While we can't always understand God's reasons, we know that he permits Satan some liberty in order to accomplish his plans. The devil's temptation caused Peter to deny Jesus three times, but Peter's repentance gave him the strength to encourage his fellow disciples. Judas' betrayal of Jesus was a key factor in the chain of events that led to his crucifixion—and ultimately to our salvation.

As believers, we need to realize that Satan is permitted to tempt us from time to time as well. If Jesus was tempted in the desert, we know that we're going to be tempted also. We don't really have to understand the reasons why. Our task is simply to resist the devil, and watch him flee (see James 4:7)! We don't have to fear the devil's tactics, because Jesus will not allow us to be tempted beyond *our power to resist* (see 1 Corinthians 10:13). We must remember that he *has* given us that power; with his grace, and the wonderful gift of our free will, we can say "no" to sin and "yes" to loving God and our brothers and sisters.

If you are failing in certain areas, ask yourself whether it is because you are relying on yourself too much. Perhaps you want to spend more time in prayer, but instead wind up in front of the television. Perhaps you try to get along better with someone, but every time they say that "certain thing," you end up losing your temper. Have you tried calling on Jesus for help? He has already defeated Satan, and his strength is all you need! He has promised never to leave or forsake you, and he's always ready to meet your need: If you choose, you can join those who are "more than conquerors" in him (Romans 8:37).

"Lord, I praise you for your great victory over the powers of darkness. Give me greater confidence in your strength, and help me to know the authority I have as your child."

Revelation 20:11–21:2

[11] Then I saw a great white throne and the one who sat on it; the earth and the heaven fled from his presence, and no place was found for them. [12]And I saw the dead, great and small, standing before the throne, and books were opened. Also another book was opened, the book of life. And the dead were judged according to their works, as

recorded in the books. ¹³And the sea gave up the dead that were in it, Death and Hades gave up the dead that were in them, and all were judged according to what they had done. ¹⁴Then Death and Hades were thrown into the lake of fire. This is the second death, the lake of fire; ¹⁵and anyone whose name was not found written in the book of life was thrown into the lake of fire.

^{21:1}Then I saw a new heaven and a new earth; for the first heaven and the first earth had passed away, and the sea was no more. ²And I saw the holy city, the new Jerusalem, coming down out of heaven from God, prepared as a bride adorned for her husband. ☙

The Book of Revelation points to the purpose of every other book in Scripture, every teaching of the church, and every undertaking of Christians all over the world. It proclaims that everything will be fulfilled in "the revelation of Jesus Christ." It tells us that a time will come when every thing that is destined to happen will be completed and when Jesus will return in glory to gather us to himself.

When all things in God's plan have been manifested, Jesus will inaugurate the glory of a new creation, a new Jerusalem, a true dwelling place for God and his bride. Reading the descriptions of the end in Revelation can overwhelm us and even make us fearful. We will, after all, one day be standing before the throne of God! Yet, we need not be concerned or troubled. This is what every work of healing is geared toward. It is what every conviction of sin, every assurance of forgiveness, and every act of Christian kindness is geared toward. From the very start of our lives, Jesus has been preparing us for the day of judgment.

Our hope in Jesus should fill us with joy and anticipation and a longing to be with him forever. When that time comes, every desire of our hearts will be fulfilled. Right now, our souls long for the courts of the Lord, but so did Jesus' when he walked the earth!

It was by staying close to his Father in obedience that Jesus was able to withstand temptation and receive strength for his journey to Jerusalem. Now, Jesus wants us to stay close to him so we will have strength for our journey to the new Jerusalem.

God longs to welcome us to the shelter of his sanctuary. Let us ask the Holy Spirit to expand our vision, to open our minds to the reality of Jesus' return and the consummation of all things. We will then stand secure before the Son of man, trusting the promises of God's word. "Blessed are those who are invited to the marriage supper of the Lamb" (Revelation 19:9).

"Father, by your Holy Spirit, heal the darkness of my mind that I may stand firm in the truth that your love has saved me. Help me to see Jesus more, triumphant over all forces of darkness and sin in the world."

Revelation 21:3-8

³And I heard a loud voice from the throne saying,
"See, the home of God is among mortals.
He will dwell with them as their God;
they will be his peoples,
and God himself will be with them;
⁴ he will wipe every tear from their eyes.
Death will be no more;
mourning and crying and pain will be no more,
for the first things have passed away."
⁵ And the one who was seated on the throne said, "See, I am making all things new." Also he said, "Write this, for these words are trustworthy and true." ⁶Then he said to me, "It is done! I am the Alpha and the Omega, the beginning and the end. To the thirsty I will give water as a gift from the spring of the water of life. ⁷Those

who conquer will inherit these things, and I will be their God and they will be my children. ⁸But as for the cowardly, the faithless, the polluted, the murderers, the fornicators, the sorcerers, the idolaters, and all liars, their place will be in the lake that burns with fire and sulfur, which is the second death."

These words about heaven are perhaps the most compelling ever written; it's the place where "death will be no more," and where we will have no more tears, crying, or pain ever again. It sounds so beautiful that we almost want to stop right there! Then a few verses further on, we're told about those who will *not* experience this beauty—and we notice that the first on the list are the "cowardly" and "faithless." Besides wondering why John starts sounding so tough all of a sudden, we might be asking a little nervously, "I wonder if I could be on this list?"

If that's what you're thinking, be thankful! That is exactly what the Holy Spirit intended! He doesn't want to scare us or to make us despair of God's mercy—that's what Satan does. The purpose of these verses is to get us to reflect *now* on the judgment that we will all face at the end of time. That's why Jesus interrupts John's vision of heaven to tell him, "Write this." He wants to be sure the readers understand that our entrance into heaven is not unconditionally guaranteed.

What is it that would keep us out of heaven? We have all sinned, but according to Revelation, the fact that we're sinners isn't the main issue. It's the "thirsty" and those who "conquer" who receive eternal life: Those who have seen their need for God's mercy, have repented, and have persevered in their faith are admitted without cost, while those who persist in their rebellion against God remain in the desert of their selfishness and sin. It's the attitude of our hearts, more than anything else, that determines where we will end up.

This very moment can be an opportunity to reflect on your walk with the Lord. Everyone has some area where he or she could do better. The trouble is, we are often so busy that we don't take the time to examine our hearts. Are you hungering and thirsting for the Lord today? If not, why not? Is it possible that the attractions of the world have dulled your hunger? Perhaps your faith has become a matter of routine, and you've grown somewhat lukewarm. Maybe there is a past memory that is convincing you that you really can't hope for any closeness with the Lord—or for an end to some pattern of sin or weakness.

Don't give up! Jesus is still the Messiah. He is still the all-powerful Lord of heaven, who can move mountains in your life. Just sit quietly in his presence today and open your heart to him. He will show you what he wants to do in you. With his strength, it really is possible to be transformed into the glorious likeness of Christ! It really is possible for each and every one of us to become the person we were created to be.

So what are you waiting for?

"Lord, I want to be set free from any self-deception concerning my life with you. Send me your gentle conviction to reveal anything that is keeping me from moving forward in my faith. Purify me with your fire, Lord, and make me a new creation!"

Revelation 21:9-21

9 Then one of the seven angels who had the seven bowls full of the seven last plagues came and said to me, "Come, I will show you the bride, the wife of the Lamb." 10And in the spirit he carried me away to a great, high mountain and showed me the holy city Jerusalem coming down out of heaven from God. 11It has the glory of God and a radiance like a very rare jewel, like jasper, clear as crystal. 12It has a great, high wall with twelve gates, and at the gates twelve angels, and on the gates are inscribed the names of the twelve tribes of the

Israelites; [13]on the east three gates, on the north three gates, on the south three gates, and on the west three gates. [14]And the wall of the city has twelve foundations, and on them are the twelve names of the twelve apostles of the Lamb.

[15] The angel who talked to me had a measuring rod of gold to measure the city and its gates and walls. [16]The city lies foursquare, its length the same as its width; and he measured the city with his rod, fifteen hundred miles; its length and width and height are equal. [17]He also measured its wall, one hundred forty-four cubits by human measurement, which the angel was using. [18]The wall is built of jasper, while the city is pure gold, clear as glass. [19]The foundations of the wall of the city are adorned with every jewel; the first was jasper, the second sapphire, the third agate, the fourth emerald, [20]the fifth onyx, the sixth carnelian, the seventh chrysolite, the eighth beryl, the ninth topaz, the tenth chrysoprase, the eleventh jacinth, the twelfth amethyst. [21]And the twelve gates are twelve pearls, each of the gates is a single pearl, and the street of the city is pure gold, transparent as glass.

We tend to think of heaven as far removed from anything we can experience on earth. Certainly, it's more glorious than we could ever imagine. And certainly, it's a place where there is nothing but joy, love, unity, and peace—unlike so much of what we experience in this world. But have you ever thought of heaven as being made of *history*? Look at how John describes the gates to the new Jerusalem: They are inscribed with the names of the twelve tribes of Israel, a people God called at a specific time to be his own, a people he called so that he could work out his specific purposes here on the earth. Likewise, the city's foundations are named for the apostles, who carried the good news of Christ's salvation to the world.

The images that John uses here tell us that the heavenly church is built on the lives of real, flesh-and-blood people—believers who chose not to take the easy way out but to walk in obedience and holiness. It is built on people like Abraham, who was called to journey far from his home when already an old man; Moses, who was afraid to speak, yet still delivered Yahweh's message to Pharaoh; and Peter, who liked doing things his way, but ended up surrendering everything to Jesus.

But it's not just the grand heroes and heroines of the faith who are the foundation of heaven. The new Jerusalem is made up of each and every believer in Christ—ordinary people like us who lived out their faith and sought to love the Lord with their lives. All these saints "in glory" faced many challenges, but they held fast to their vision of what God had in mind for them.

Today, we will be given many choices: to spend time with Jesus in prayer, or to hurry out the door without connecting with the Lord; to listen to someone who needs our help, or to make a hasty excuse and walk away; to give away some of our time and treasure, or to keep it for ourselves. Although our actions may seem insignificant, they are actually the very building blocks of heaven—the daily choices we make for God that help us, little by little, to become more like him. So when you feel tempted to discouragement, remember that you are important to him. Together, we are all the living stones that he is using to build up his church now—and for all eternity!

"Lord, how deep are your designs! I praise you for making me a part of your great plan of salvation. Use me, Lord, to bring others to your heavenly city!"

Revelation 21:22-27

²² I saw no temple in the city, for its temple is the Lord God the Almighty and the Lamb. ²³And the city has no need of sun or moon to shine on it, for the glory of God is its light, and its lamp is the Lamb. ²⁴The nations will walk by its light, and the kings of the earth will bring their glory into it. ²⁵Its gates will never be shut by day— and there will be no night there. ²⁶People will bring into it the glory and the honor of the nations. ²⁷But nothing unclean will enter it, nor anyone who practices abomination or falsehood, but only those who are written in the Lamb's book of life.

Doesn't it strike you as a bit odd that heaven is described here as having no Temple? It's like imagining Rome without St. Peter's Basilica. Shouldn't there be some focal point for the people's worship? Shouldn't there be some monument to and reminder of the glory of the Lord?

In the Old Testament, the Temple was the most sacred of places. It was the place where the glory of Yahweh dwelt, where sacrifices were offered for the well-being of the people. It was the place where the prophet Isaiah had his overwhelming vision of the throne of God, and where the high priest went every year to atone for the sins of all the people (Isaiah 6:1-4; Leviticus 16). How could there not be some heavenly equivalent of the Temple? Yet this is but one more sign of God's immense and glorious plan for us.

In ancient times, or even in our own day, a temple or church is vital for the identity of the people. The world all around may be filled with innumerable vices and sins, but the temple or church stands apart. At least this place remains holy and serves as a reminder of God's presence.

But in heaven, we won't need a temple or a church—or even a tabernacle with the Real Presence of Christ in the Eucharist. Why?

Because the glory of God will suffuse everything. In heaven, there will be nothing unclean, unholy, or profane at all. There will be no need for a "sacred space" because the Lord won't be hidden anymore!

John tells us that in heaven there will be no sun or moon either, because the glory of God will be all the light the city will ever need. The veil of this fallen world will be torn away. Every obstacle to the light of God, every shadow cast by sin, fear, pride, or unbelief will be gone. Nothing will stand between God and his people.

St. Irenaeus, a second-century church father, once famously said that the glory of God is man fully alive. In heaven, we will all be "fully alive" in Christ. Every trace of sin and death will be wiped away, and we will be so filled with Christ that we ourselves will radiate his goodness, his love, and his glory to one another. In a sense, we ourselves will provide the light of heaven!

All of these images give us a sense of the perfection and completeness of heaven, but they also give us a sense of our calling here on earth. Rather than merely waiting for heaven to be revealed, each one of us is called to bring heaven down to earth. We are called to be the light of Jesus' love and presence to the world. We are called to live as temples of the Holy Spirit—as a people who reflect the holiness and glory that is available to everyone who embraces the gospel. So what are you waiting for? You are far more powerful than you think!

"Jesus, give me a greater confidence of who I am in you. By your Holy Spirit, fill me with a vision of heaven that propels me into this world that you love so dearly. Make me your ambassador, Lord, so that everyone around me will learn to walk by your light—the light of God that shines from me."

Revelation 22:1-5

¹ Then the angel showed me the river of the water of life, bright as crystal, flowing from the throne of God and of the Lamb ²through the middle of the street of the city. On either side of the river is the tree of life with its twelve kinds of fruit, producing its fruit each month; and the leaves of the tree are for the healing of the nations. ³Nothing accursed will be found there any more. But the throne of God and of the Lamb will be in it, and his servants will worship him; ⁴they will see his face, and his name will be on their foreheads. ⁵And there will be no more night; they need no light of lamp or sun, for the Lord God will be their light, and they will reign forever and ever.

Why do we find it so difficult to receive gifts? So often, we can feel that if someone is generous with us, we owe them something. We have to "pay them back." It's hard to receive a gift graciously and believe that the giver just wanted to express love for us. All of the images that John uses at the end of the Book of Revelation speak in one way or another about God ministering to his people, and about his people receiving his ministry eagerly and gratefully.

This is the heart of the gospel. It is all about a generous God giving to a needy people. It is not about good people doing good and being rewarded. It is not about a list of rules and regulations that make us acceptable to God when we die. The gospel is about being made right, being forgiven, being loved without condition by God. These free gifts from God are ones we should gratefully accept, saying simply, "Thank you, Father," as he releases us from the power of sin.

The more we learn to receive from Jesus, the closer he draws us to himself, and the more fully we are compelled to obey his commands and to love one another. It may seem so difficult to receive from Jesus. We can feel unworthy and sinful. We can believe that there is no way he could possibly love us so deeply. But Jesus loves all of us, even the worst of sinners. He stands ready to give his love in fullness, no matter who we are or what we have done.

In order to accept his gift of love, we need to be on guard against anything that keeps us from receiving it. "Be on guard so that your hearts are not weighed down with dissipation and drunkenness and worries of this life" (Luke 21:34). If we are not alert, we might miss out on Jesus' presence. A lack of vigilance can block the flow of grace and cause us to become dull to the Spirit's voice. Let us try every day to be open to Jesus' presence and to accept gratefully all that he wants to give us.

"Jesus, I give myself to you. I come to you to receive all you want to give me. I won't focus on what I can bring you today. Instead I will focus on receiving your love and your guidance."

The Spirit and the Bride Say, "Come!"

Revelation 22:6-21

THE SPIRIT AND THE BRIDE SAY, "COME!"

The Spirit and the Bride Say, "Come!"
Revelation 22:6-21

Revelation 22:6-15

6 And he said to me, "These words are trustworthy and true, for the Lord, the God of the spirits of the prophets, has sent his angel to show his servants what must soon take place."

7 "See, I am coming soon! Blessed is the one who keeps the words of the prophecy of this book."

8 I, John, am the one who heard and saw these things. And when I heard and saw them, I fell down to worship at the feet of the angel who showed them to me; 9but he said to me, "You must not do that! I am a fellow servant with you and your comrades the prophets, and with those who keep the words of this book. Worship God!"

10 And he said to me, "Do not seal up the words of the prophecy of this book, for the time is near. 11Let the evildoer still do evil, and the filthy still be filthy, and the righteous still do right, and the holy still be holy."

12 "See, I am coming soon; my reward is with me, to repay according to everyone's work. 13I am the Alpha and the Omega, the first and the last, the beginning and the end."

14 Blessed are those who wash their robes, so that they will have the right to the tree of life and may enter the city by the gates. 15Outside are the dogs and sorcerers and fornicators and murderers and idolaters, and everyone who loves and practices falsehood.

Throughout Scripture, God shows us that there is indeed "a time for every matter under heaven" (Ecclesiastes 3:1). In one of the stories in the Book of Daniel, we read that Daniel receives several prophecies and visions. He is shown events that are truly "apocalyptic," signifying not only the defeat of Israel's enemies but also a future for the world. Daniel asks when all of these things will happen, but the angel commands him to "keep the words secret and the book sealed until the time of the end" (Daniel 12:4). Here, at the end of Revelation, we see that John is told just the opposite: "Do not seal up the words of the prophecy of this book" (Revelation 22:10).

Why is John told to proclaim what Daniel was told to concel? Because the time is near (Revelation 22:10). John is making a deliberate reference to the Book of Daniel because he wants his readers to know that the fulfillment of what Daniel spoke of—the coming day of freedom for God's people—is just around the corner. He is writing to his fellow believers who, like the faithful in Daniel's time, are suffering persecution under an oppressive ruler and wondering when they will finally see the day of the Lord. He is telling them not to give up hope, because their redemption is at hand.

We can be thankful that John did as the angel commanded, because now we, too, can be inspired and renewed by his vision of God's ultimate triumph over evil. However, as inspiring as this message is, it is also challenging. We have inherited John's mission as well as his vision. And really, it's nothing other than the gospel mission—something we are supposed to proclaim from the rooftops, not "seal up"! We are called to give our witness to the world that the kingdom of God is at hand and that everyone can live in the age to come right now, by accepting the grace that Jesus is offering us.

Do you know what time it is? We are much closer to the day of Jesus' return than John was, so it's time to be spreading our faith. What specific revelation has God given to you? You may not have visionary gifts like John's, but we all have a talent that we can use to bring Christ into our surroundings. We all have a testimony of how he has touched our lives. And we all know at least one person who needs what we have to give: "For I tell you that many prophets and kings desired to see what you see, but did not see it, and to hear what you hear, but did not hear it" (Luke 10:24). So don't seal up the vision of the gospel. Announce it far and wide!

"Lord, give me a zeal to share your word with my brothers and sisters. Burn away any fear or complacency that may have settled in my heart, and give me the boldness to speak your truth in love!"

Revelation 22:16-21

[16] "It is I, Jesus, who sent my angel to you with this testimony for the churches. I am the root and the descendant of David, the bright morning star."
[17] The Spirit and the bride say, "Come."
And let everyone who hears say, "Come."
And let everyone who is thirsty come.
Let anyone who wishes take the water of life as a gift.
[18] I warn everyone who hears the words of the prophecy of this book: if anyone adds to them, God will add to that person the plagues described in this book; [19]if anyone takes away from the words of the book of this prophecy, God will take away that person's share in the tree of life and in the holy city, which are described in this book.
[20] The one who testifies to these things says, "Surely I am coming soon."
Amen. Come, Lord Jesus!
[21] The grace of the Lord Jesus be with all the saints. Amen.

Come, Lord Jesus! (22:20)

Sometimes when you read a novel or a mystery story, you get impatient, and you skip to the end to see what happens. Once you find the ending, you don't always have to go back and read the rest of the book, because you can more or less understand the entire work. In one sense—although we would miss a lot—we can do that with the Book of Revelation, by reading the very last sentence before John says farewell: "Come, Lord Jesus!"

This short sentence gives us a capsule summary of what Revelation is all about. It's not just a footnote or an afterthought. It's a cry of longing, hope, and confidence—a cry of faith that expresses everything John has been saying throughout this book. First of all, it shows the deep longing that John and his fellow believers had for Jesus Christ, the faithful and true one, to bring the justice of his kingdom to this earth and destroy the influences of paganism and materialism that were corrupting their society.

Second, it shows these believers' hope that, in spite of the persecution they were enduring, Jesus would come back one day and take them to his dwelling place, the "new Jerusalem," where they would live with him forever, free from all pain and suffering. Facing the possibility of martyrdom, they gained a heavenly perspective on their lives and a strong desire to be united with Jesus. Their hope was not in what they saw but in "a building from God, a house not made with hands, eternal in the heavens" (2 Corinthians 5:1).

Come, Lord Jesus! This is more than a plea. It also reveals the believers' great confidence that not only would God come in the future, he was with them already! Through the baptismal water of life that Jesus offers to everyone, they were already a part of his kingdom. They were already being prepared as the spotless bride who would soon be ready for the marriage supper of the Lamb. Perhaps that's why the early Christians used these very words (*Maranatha* in Aramaic) in their liturgies. Perhaps that's also why some of them even read John's letter aloud before they celebrated the Eucharist!

Though many centuries have elapsed since Revelation was written, we have the same longing that its first readers had. We all want Jesus to come into our hearts, even as we await his final return to earth. The next time you are at Mass and you hear the prayer, "Lord Jesus, come in glory!" remember that you are about to receive just what God promised you in the Book of Revelation. You are not just getting a little glimpse of heaven, you are getting the *reality* of heaven, in the body and blood of Jesus Christ, our "hope of glory" (Colossians 1:27). May we be generous receivers of this blessing always and everywhere!

"Lord, make me ready for your coming! May this be the hour that I turn my life completely over to you. Come, Lord Jesus, and transform me into your trusting and obedient servant!"

The New Testament Devotional Commentary Series From The Word Among Us Press

Enjoy praying through the New Testament with these faith-filled commentaries. Each commentary includes the complete Scripture text, followed by a devotional meditation based on the passage, along with introductory articles by trusted Catholic biblical scholars.

Matthew
306 pages, $18.00
Item # BMATT7

Mark
194 pages, $16.00
Item # BMARK8

Luke
290 pages, $18.00
Item # BLUKE9

John
232 pages, $18.00
Item # BJOHN0

Acts of the Apostles
221 pages, $18.00
Item # BACTS1

Romans and Galatians
181 pages, $16.00
Item # BROME2

I & II Corinthians
200 pages, $16.00
Item # BCORE3

Ephesians through Thessalonians
176 pages, $16.00
Item # BEPHE4

1 Timothy through Hebrews
232 pages, $16.00
Item # BTIME5

The Catholic Epistles
184 pages, $16.00
Item # BJAME6

Revelation
168 pages, $15.00
Item # BREVE7

To order these and other fine books from The Word Among Us Press, log on to www.wordamongus.org, call 1-800-775-9673, or visit your local Catholic bookstore.